THE CASE FOR CLERICAL CELIBACY

ALFONS MARIA CARDINAL STICKLER

THE CASE FOR CLERICAL CELIBACY

Its Historical Development and Theological Foundations

Translated by Father Brian Ferme

IGNATIUS PRESS   SAN FRANCISCO

Title of the German original:
Der Klerikerzölibat
Seine Entwicklungsgeschichte und seine theologischen Grundlagen
© 1993 Kral Verlag, Abensberg, Germany

© 1995 Ignatius Press, San Francisco
ISBN 0-89870-533-9
Library of Congress catalogue number 94-79297
Printed in the United States of America

CONTENTS

INTRODUCTION

IN THE ONGOING DISCUSSION on clerical celibacy in the Catholic Church, which in recent years has been markedly intensified, one regularly hears a variety of divergent opinions in both the Western and Eastern Churches, particularly with regard to its origins and development. These opinions range from, on the one hand, a belief in its divine origins to, on the other, the view that clerical celibacy is merely an ecclesiastical institution especially of the stricter discipline in the Latin Church. Those holding the latter view often say that the obligation to celibacy can first be verified from the fourth century, while others claim that celibacy was introduced only at the beginning of the second millennium, above all by the Second Lateran Council in 1139. These various opinions, marked both by their considerable divergence and by the various reasons put forward to support them, reflect a particular lack of certainty in our knowledge of the relevant facts, of the pertinent ecclesiastical regulations, and especially of the reasons for clerical celibacy. This uncertainty, as remarks on the subject show, extends into and up ecclesiastical circles.

In order to arrive at a correct understanding of this much-discussed institution, it is first of all necessary to clarify the pertinent facts and the regulations of the

Church from the beginning until the present time and to explore the theological reasons for celibacy. This can only be done, of course, on the basis of a knowledge of the relevant sources and of current scholarship if our presentation is to be accepted as valid and scientifically credible. In recent years there have been a number of important studies devoted to the history of celibacy in both the East and the West, and this clearly has particular relevance to our study. These studies have either not yet penetrated the general consciousness or they have been hushed up if they were capable of influencing that consciousness in undesirable ways.[1]

---

[1] In the first place, reference should be made to three fundamental studies: Christian Cochini, S.J., *Origines apostoliques du célibat*, Le Sycomore (Paris: Lethielleux, 1981); English trans.: *Apostolic Origins of Priestly Celibacy* (San Francisco: Ignatius Press, 1990). Roman Cholij, *Clerical Celibacy in East and West* (contains above all the explanation of the development of celibacy in the Eastern Churches) (Leominster: Fowler Wright Books, 1988). Filippo Liotta, *La Continenza dei Chierici nel pensiero canonistico classico (da Graziano a Gregorio IX)*, Quaderni di Studi Senesi 24 (Milan: Giuffrè, 1971).

Further recent general publications include: J. Coppens, ed., *Sacerdoce et Célibat*, Bibliotheca Ephemeridum Theol. Lovanien 28 (1971) (this includes: Alfons M. Stickler, "L'Évolution de la discipline du célibat dans l'Église en Occident de la fin de l'âge patristique au concile de Trente", 373–442). There is an English (1972) and Italian (1975) translation of this general work of collected essays. Roger Gryson, *Les Origines du célibat ecclésiastique* (Gembloux: Duculot, 1970). Georg Denzler, "Das Papsttum und der Amtszölibat", in *Päpste und Papsttum* 5, no. 1 (Stuttgart, 1973), 5, no. 2 (1976). Martin Boelens, *Die Klerikerehe in der Gesetzgebung der Kirche unter besonderer Berücksichtigung der Strafe: Von den Anfängen der Kirche bis zum Jahre 1139* (Paderborn,

The present synthetic presentation will be accompanied by a scholarly apparatus which necessarily will have to limit itself to the essentials. Nevertheless, it will not only allow the possibility of examining more closely the various affirmations made but also will enable further detailed study.

In order to understand the historical development of celibacy in the Western and Eastern Churches, the present study will begin with an analysis of the actual concept of clerical celibacy which necessarily lies at the basis of the respective obligations that it imposes. In addition, in order that our conclusions be solidly founded, it will be necessary to provide an outline of the method which a proper treatment of this argument demands. The final part will be devoted to the theological foundations of clerical celibacy, which are demanded with ever-increasing urgency.

1969). Id., "Die Klerikerehe in der kirchlichen Gesetzgebung vom II. Laterankonzil bis zum Konzil von Basel", in: *Ius Sacrum* (Festschrift für Klaus Mörsdorf), (Paderborn, 1969) 593–614. Id., "Die Klerikerehe in der kirchlichen Gesetzgebung zwischen den Konzilien Basel und Trient", in: *Archiv für katholisches Kirchenrecht* 138 (1969): 62–81. A. Franzen, *Zölibat und Priesterehe in der katholischen Reform des 16. Jahrhunderts* (Münster, 1969; 2d ed., 1970). Alfons M. Stickler, "La continenza dei Diaconi specialmente nel primo millennio della Chiesa", in: *Salesianum* 26 (1964): 275–302. Id., "Tratti salienti nella storia del celibato", in: *Sacra Doctrina* 60 (1970): 585–620.

I

CONCEPT AND METHOD

1 THE FIRST AND MOST IMPORTANT PREREQUISITE for a knowledge of the historical development of any institution is the proper understanding of the meaning of the concepts on which it is based. For ecclesiastical celibacy, we have a particularly clear and concise reference in the writings of one of the greatest of the Decretists—commentators on Gratian's *Decretum* —who around 1140 collected and explained all the material concerning the juridical tradition of the first millennium of the Church. This Decretist is Huguccio of Pisa (d. 1210), who in his *Summa* on the *Decretum*, composed around 1190, began his treatment of celibacy with these words: "In hac Distinctione incipit (Gratianus) tractare specialiter de continentia clericorum, scilicet quam debent observare *in non contrahendo matrimonio* et *in non utendo contracto*."[1]

---

[1] [In this section (Gratian) begins specifically to treat the clerical celibacy, i.e., which clerics are bound to observe *in not contracting marriage* and *in not exercising the rights of marriage*.] Dist. 27, dict.

11

A reading of this text clearly indicates a double obligation with respect to celibacy: not to marry and, if previously married, not to use the rights of marriage. In addition, it is clear that even in this period, namely, the end of the twelfth century, there were clerics in major orders who had been married prior to ordination. In fact we know from the Scriptures that the ordination of married men was a normal enough event. Saint Paul, in writing to his disciples Titus and Timothy, prescribed that such candidates could be married only once.[2] We know at least that Saint Peter was certainly married, since Peter said to his Master: "What about us? We left all we had to follow you." To this, Christ responded (Saint Luke): "I tell you solemnly, there is no one who has left house, *wife*, brothers, parents or *children* for the sake of the kingdom of God, who will not be given repayment many times over in this present time and, in the world to come, eternal life."[3]

Here we clearly already have the first obligation of clerical celibacy, namely, the commitment to continence in the use of marriage after ordination. The real meaning of celibacy, which today is in general almost totally forgotten but which in the first millennium and

introd. ad v. quod autem. See *Studia Gratiana*, ed. by J. Forchielli and Alfons M. Stickler, vols. 1–3 (Bologna, 1953ff.)

[2] 1 Tim 3:2 and 3:12; Titus 1:6.

[3] Mt 19:27–30; Mk 10:20–21; Lk 18:28–30.

beyond was well known, consists in this: complete abstinence with respect to the procreation of children even within the context of marriage. In fact all the first laws written on celibacy speak of this prohibition, that is, of the further procreation of children, a point which will be convincingly documented in the second part of this study. This indicates that, despite the fact that many clerics were already married before their ordination, they were nevertheless held to this particular obligation before they could be ordained. In the beginning, the actual prohibition to marry remained somewhat in the background. It emerged only later when the Church imposed the prohibition against marriage on those celibates from whom virtually all the candidates for sacred orders were exclusively recruited.

To complete this initial understanding of celibacy, which from the very beginning was correctly termed "continence", we must immediately note that married candidates could approach sacred orders and renounce the use of marriage only with the consent of their wife. The reason for this lies in the fact that, on the basis of the sacrament that had already been received, the wife had an inalienable right to the use of the valid (and consummated) marriage, which in itself was indissoluble. We will consider the complex problems that resulted from this renunciation in the second part of this work.

2. The second prerequisite for a correct understanding of the origins and development of clerical celibacy —which, given what has just been described, should be called sexual "continence"—concerns the research method to be applied to this question. This is of particular importance given the number of opinions about the origins and first developments of the obligation to continence. Frequently they are the result of a flawed methodology in both their analysis and their explanation of the problem.

In the first place, it is necessary to underline that every area of study has what in general might be termed its own proper object and methodology, which are strictly connected to one another. It is also true that for related areas of study there are common rules that must be observed and applied in actual research. Thus, for example, in historical research, one cannot disregard the rules that are fundamental for a preliminary analysis of the sources and which in turn establish their authenticity and integrity and thereby their intrinsic value. In other words, how credible they are and what probative value can be assigned to them. Only on this basis can one then correctly consider and evaluate the evidence and assertions contained in the particular documents. Thus a proper hermeneutic and a correct interpretation of the sources can only be established on this basis: by taking into account their authenticity, integrity, credibility and particular worth.

In addition to these general methodological prerequisites, it is also necessary to apply, however, the specific method required in every particular field of research. Hence, a competent history of philosophy presupposes an adequate knowledge of philosophy; a history of theology, a knowledge of theology. Likewise, the history of medicine and mathematics requires a sufficient knowledge of these two sciences. Thus, for a history of law, a knowledge of law and of its particular and proper methodology is also clearly fundamental.

Given this, we need to be conscious of the fact that the history of celibacy implies, with respect to its content and development, an understanding of both the law of the Church and of Catholic theology. Therefore, in establishing a correct hermeneutic of the relevant historical evidence (documents and facts), serious consideration must be paid to the method proper to both canon law and theology. While at first sight these observations may appear somewhat abstract, I would like immediately to demonstrate their meaning and necessity by applying them to a concrete question relative to our study.

At the end of the last century, a well-known and somewhat heated discussion took place about the origins of clerical celibacy. Gustav Bickell, son of a lawyer and himself an orientalist, traced its origins to an apostolic rule by appealing above all to evidence from the East. Franz X. Funk, a well-known historian of the early Church, responded to Bickell claiming that this could not be affirmed since the first law on celibacy could be found only at the beginning of the fourth century. After a series of further exchanges in various articles on the question, Bickell made no reply, while Funk continued to publish his views without receiving any response from his adversary. He did receive, however, the significant agreement of other leading scholars, such as E. F. Vacandard and H. Leclercq. Their influence and authority in combination with their tendency to express their views in widely disseminated works helped to assure Funk's theory an almost universal acceptance that endures even today.[4]

Taking into consideration what has been stated above concerning the need to follow clear methodological

---

[4] Gustav Bickell, "Der Cölibat eine apostolische Anordnung", in: *Zeitschrift für katholische Theologie* 2 (1878): 26–64. Id., "Der Cölibat dennoch eine apostolische Anordnung", in: *Zeitschrift für katholische Theologie* 3 (1879): 792–99. Franz Xaver Funk, "Der Cölibat keine apostolische Anordnung", in: *Tübinger theologische Quartalschrift* 61 (1879): 208–47. Id., "Der Cölibat noch lange keine apostolische Anordnung", in: *Tübinger theologische Quartalschrift* 62 (1880): 202–21. Id., "Cölibat und Priesterehe im Christlichen Altertum", in: *Kirchengeschichtliche Abhandlungen und Untersuchungen* 1 (1897) 121–55. Elphège-Florent Vacandard, "Les Origines du célibat ecclésiastique", in: *Études de critique et d'histoire religieuse*, 1st ser. (Paris, 1905; 5th ed.: Paris, 1913), 71–120. Id., art. "Célibat", in: *Dictionnaire de théologie catholique* 2 (Paris, 1905): 2068–88. Henri Leclercq, "La Législation conciliaire relative au célibat ecclésiastique", in the extended French edition of *Conciliengeschichte*, by Carl Josef v. Hefele, vol. 2, part 2 (Paris, 1908), appendix 6, 1321–48. Id., art. "Célibat", in: *Dictionnaire d'Archéologie chrétienne et de liturgie* 2 (Paris, 1908): 2802–32.

principles for this type of research, it must be pointed out that Funk, both in the development and presentation of his results, did not apply the general principles necessary for a critical study and appreciation of the sources. He accepted as one of his principal arguments against Bickell the spurious story of the monk-bishop Paphnutius of Egypt at the Council of Nicaea (325). This was surprising in such an eminent scholar, given the fact that even before Funk a critical appraisal of the sources had repeatedly concluded that this episode was false. This has also been confirmed by contemporary research, as will be seen when we return to the question in our discussion of the Council of Nicaea. Funk made a still greater error when he asserted that the official obligation to celibacy first began only with the appearance of a specific written law on the topic. The same mistake must also have been made by Vacandard, a historian of theology, and Leclercq, a historian of councils.

Every historian of law knows (as Hans Kelsen, one of the most authoritative legal theorists of this century, has clearly affirmed) that an identification between law in the general sense and norms (rules, statutes) is mistaken, *ius et lex*. Law (*ius*) is any obligatory legal norm, whether it be established orally or handed on by means of a custom or already expressed in writing. A norm (*lex*), on the other hand, is any regulation established in a written form and legitimately promulgated.

It is a particular characteristic of law, explained in

every history on the topic, that the origin of every legal system consists in oral traditions and in the transmission of customary norms which only slowly receive a fixed written form. Thus it was only after centuries and for various sociological reasons that the Romans formulated in writing the law of the Twelve Tables. The German peoples only compiled their popular juridical system and customs in written form after many centuries of their actual existence. Up to that time, their law was unwritten and was handed on orally. No one would thereby affirm that, on this basis, their law (*ius*) was not obligatory and that its observance was left to the free will of the individual.

Like the legal system of any large community, that of the early Church consisted for the greater part in regulations and obligations which were handed on orally, particularly during the three centuries of persecution, which made it difficult to fix them in writing. On the other hand, the Church, to a greater degree than other new societies, had written elements of law from the very beginning. Evidence of this can be found in Scripture. Saint Paul in his Second Letter to the Thessalonians (2:15) wrote: "Stand firm, then, brothers, and keep the traditions that we taught you, whether by word of mouth or by letter." Without doubt we are dealing here with obligatory regulations which had been given, as is said explicitly, not only in writing but also handed on orally. Anyone, therefore, who claims that only those norms are obligatory which have been written down fails to do justice to the cognitive method proper to the domain of legal history.

Further, in considering the correct method to arrive at an understanding of the theological foundations of clerical continence, one must give explicit consideration to the fact that alongside the disciplinary and hence juridical material, we are also dealing with a charism which is intimately connected with the Church and with Christ. This clearly implies that the theological foundations can be understood and analyzed only in the light of revelation and of theological reflection.

It is now known that medieval theology gave little independent study to subjects connected with the law and discipline. Rather, it made its own the discussions and the conclusions of the classic canonists, who were flourishing in this period, especially through the work of the glossators. The historians of medieval theology have explicitly identified this phenomenon,[5] and a glance at the works of the greatest of the medieval scholastics, Saint Thomas Aquinas, obviously confirms their findings. This is surely the principal reason why clerical celibacy or continence has not been satisfactorily studied by theology itself, that is, by following its own proper method based on revelation and its sources. True, this lacuna has already been partially filled, but a far more profound understanding of the

[5] Cf. Arthur Michael Landgraf, "Diritto canonico e teologia nel sec. XII", in: *Studia Gratiana* 1:371–413.

theological foundations for our subject is urgently required. This all-too-justified demand will be accommodated in the final part of this work.

II

THE DEVELOPMENT
IN THE LATIN CHURCH

G IVEN THESE NECESSARY CONSIDERATIONS concerning concept and method, our first task is to trace the development of clerical continence in the Latin Church. Taking into account the evidence to hand, we must begin with the Council of Elvira. In the first decade of the fourth century, bishops and priests of the Spanish Church assembled in the diocese of Elvira near Granada. Their aim was to restore legal unity and stability to the Church in that region of Spain which belonged to the western part of the empire and which under Constantius had enjoyed a period of greater stability. During the persecution of the Christian religion in the preceding period, there is evidence of a breakdown in more than one area of Christian life which had seriously undermined the observance of ecclesiastical discipline. The Council promulgated eighty-one canons which in general concerned themselves with those important areas of ecclesiastical life that had been in need of clarification and renewal. The canons also aimed at reaffirming the ancient discipline and establishing new norms that were considered necessary.

As has already been noted, Canon 33 of this Council contained the first regulation on celibacy. Under the title: "Concerning bishops and ministers (of the altar) who must live in abstinence with their wives", we find the following text:

> It has seemed good absolutely to forbid the bishops, the priests, and the deacons, i.e., all the clerics engaged in service at the altar, to have [sexual] relations with their wives and procreate children; should anyone do so, let him be excluded from the honor of the clergy.

Canon 27 had already established a prohibition forbidding unrelated women to live with bishops and other clerics. Only a sister or a daughter, consecrated a virgin, could do so, but on no account another woman.[1]

From these first important legislative texts a number of conclusions can be drawn: many, if not the greater part, of the higher clergy of the Spanish Church at that time were *viri probati*, that is to say, men married before their ordination as deacons, priests or bishops. However, after having received sacred orders, they were obliged to a complete renunciation of every further use of marriage, that is, they had to observe com-

---

[1] Hermann Theodor Bruns, *Canones Apostolorum et Conciliorum sæc. IV–VII*, 2 (Berlin, 1839): 5–6.

plete continence. If we consider the general aim of the Council of Elvira alongside the concept of law, which in that period of Spanish history was dominated by Roman legal culture, it is impossible to hold that in canon 33 (along with canon 27) we have a new law. It was instead a reaction to the prevalent nonobservance of a traditional obligation that was well known, and to which now was also added a sanction: either observe the obligation that had been undertaken or renounce the clerical office. Clearly if this had been an innovation—which in effect included a retroactive sanction against an acquired right—it would have caused a storm of protest against what would have been a clear infringement of rights. This was already clearly understood by Pius XI in his encyclical on the priesthood when he affirmed that this written law presupposed a previous praxis.[2]

Having noted this important legal text from Elvira, we must immediately turn to another of even greater significance, one which remains a crucial point of reference in our study. It concerns a binding declaration found for the first time in canon 2 of the African Council of 390, repeated in successive African councils, and which finally was inserted into the *Codex Canonum Ecclesiæ Africanæ*. The text is as follows.

> That the chastity of the Levites and priests must be preserved.

[2] *Acta Apostolicæ Sedis* (AAS) 28 (Rome, 1936): 25.

Bishop Epigonius . . . says: The rule of continence and chastity had been discussed in a previous council. Let it [now] be taught with more emphasis what are the three ranks that, by virtue of their consecration, are under the same obligation of chastity, i.e., the bishop, the priest and the deacon, and let them be instructed to keep their purity.

Bishop Genetlius says: As was previously said, it is fitting that the holy bishops and priests of God as well as the Levites, i.e., those who are in the service of the divine sacraments, observe perfect continence, so that they may obtain in all simplicity what they are asking from God; what the apostles taught and what antiquity itself observed, let us also endeavor to keep.

The bishops declared unanimously: It pleases us all that bishop, priest and deacon, guardians of purity, abstain from [conjugal intercourse] with their wives, so that those who serve at the altar may keep a perfect chastity.[3]

This declaration of the Council of Carthage suggests that even in the African Church a large number of the higher clergy, if not the majority, were married before their ordination. On the other hand, after their ordination they were bound to live in continence. This obligation arose on the basis of the ordination received and service at the altar. Further, it is explicitly stated that this is a teaching of the apostles, that it is an

---

[3] "Concilia Africæ a. 345–525", ed. by C. Munier, in: *Corpus Christianorum*, Series Latina 149 (Turnhout, 1974): 13.

observance of the past tradition (*antiquitas*) and that it has been unanimously confirmed by the whole African Church.

We need to understand that the African Church was particularly conscious of and open to the tradition of the ancient Church, a point that is specifically illustrated by a dispute with Rome which was also dealt with by this African Council. The priest Apiarius had been excommunicated by his bishop. He appealed to Rome, which accepted his appeal on the basis of a canon from Nicaea, which is supposed to have authorized the right of appeal to Rome. The African bishops, however, declared themselves in solidarity with their fellow bishop and claimed that they did not know of the existence of this canon from Nicaea. These questions, which were discussed in various meetings of the African bishops in which delegates from Rome also participated, are now known to us as the "*canones in causa Apiarii*."[4] The Africans asserted that in their list of the Nicaean canons they could not find the specific canon under discussion. They sent legates to Alexandria, Antioch and Constantinople to obtain further information, but even in these Eastern cities nothing was known of this particular Nicaean canon. The error on the part of Rome can be explained by the fact that the canons of the Council of Sardica had been added to those of Nicaea. The president of the Coun-

[4] Ibid., 149:98 ff.

cil of Sardica (342), which had again dealt with the
Arian question, was Hosius of Cordoba, who had also
presided over the Council of Nicaea. This led Rome to
consider the disciplinary canons of Sardica, which had
been added to those of Nicaea, as actually Nicaean.
In fact, this canon on appeals to Rome had actually
been decided upon at Sardica (canon 3). The African
Church therefore did not have great difficulty in prov-
ing to Pope Zosimus the erroneous attribution of this
canon to the Council of Nicaea.

Bishop Aurelius of Carthage was president at the
principal sitting, held on May 25, 419, that dealt with
this question. Other participants included the legate
from Rome, Faustinus of Fermo, along with two Roman priests, Philippus and Azellus, and 240 African
bishops, among whom were Augustine of Hippo and
Alypius of Tagaste. The president introduced the discussions with these words: "We have here before us
the copies of the provisions that our Fathers have
brought with them from Nicaea. We have kept them
intact, and we will also preserve the further deliberations which will be signed by us." The symbol of faith
in the Trinity [the Creed] was then pronounced by all
the Council Fathers.

After that the text concerning clerical continence
from the Council of 390, which had been recited by
Epigonius and Genetlius, was now recited again by
Aurelius. Then the papal delegate, Faustinus, under
the rubric: "Concerning the grades of sacred orders

that must abstain [from conjugal relations] with their wives", added: "It pleases us that the bishops, priests and deacons, in other words, those who touch the sacred mysteries, guardians of chastity, abstain [from conjugal relations] with their wives." To this all the bishops responded: "We agree that all those who serve at the altar should keep perfect chastity."[5]

On the basis of the tradition of the African Church, other norms were reread and confirmed. Among these we find at canon 25 a text of the president Aurelius:

As we have dealt with certain clerics, especially lectors, as regards continence with their wives, I would add, very dear brothers, what was confirmed in many synods, that the subdeacons who touch the sacred mysteries, and also the deacons, priests and bishops, in conformity with the ordinances concerning them, will abstain from their wives "as if they did not have one"; if they do not do so, they will be rejected from any ecclesiastical function. As to the other clerics, they will be compelled to do so only at an advanced age. The whole synod said: What your holiness has regulated in justice, we confirm because it is worthy of the priesthood and pleasing to God.[6]

We have quoted at length this evidence from the African Church at the end of the fourth century and the beginning of the fifth because of its fundamental importance. From these texts there is clear evidence

[5] Ibid., 149:133f.
[6] Ibid., 149:142.

of a tradition that is based not only on a general conviction, which no one doubted, but also on solid doc-
umentary evidence. In this period one still finds in the
archives of the African Church the original acts that
the Fathers had brought with them from the Council of Nicaea. Among them were norms on clerical
celibacy. The African Fathers affirmed and reasserted
them with a determination similar to that by which
they had challenged the error or oversight of the Roman Church that had attributed the canons of Sardica
to Nicaea.

It is clear from all this that the universal Church,
made up of various parts in communion with one another—Rome and Italy, Spain, Africa, Alexandria, Antioch, Constantinople—was conscious of a common
tradition. In other words, the tradition of the apostolic origins of clerical celibacy and its observance from
the very beginning, which had been explicitly and repeatedly affirmed by the African Church, even to the
extent of imposing sanctions against those contraven-
ing it, would certainly not have been so generally accepted if it had not been based on a fact that was well
known. We also have clear proof of this from the Eastern Church, to which we will return.

In the evidence from the African Church concerning celibacy, we have already noted an authoritative
confirmation on the part of Rome. The papal legate
Faustinus had clearly indicated the full agreement of
Rome on the question. Under Pope Siricius, Rome

transmitted the decisions of the Roman Synod of 386 to the bishops of Africa. They included a number of apostolic regulations which had fallen into oblivion but were now reconfirmed. This letter had been read at the Council of Thelepte (Thelense?) in 418. The last part of it (canon 9) deals with clerical continence.[7]

With this document we come to a second cluster of evidence on celibacy which is undoubtedly of greater significance, not only because it reflects the tradition observed in the universal Church, but also because it illustrates, through the testimony and provisions of the Popes, further developments in the observance of clerical celibacy.

A general indication of the importance of the position of Rome on any question, and consequently also on that concerning celibacy, is found in Saint Irenaeus. Being a disciple of Saint Polycarp, he was heir to the Johannine tradition, which he handed on to the Church of Europe as bishop of Lyons from 178. In his principal work, *Against the Heresies*, he states that the apostolic tradition is preserved in the Church of Rome, founded by the Apostles Peter and Paul, and that all other Churches must agree with it.[8] This same principle can also be applied to the tradition of clerical continence.

The first explicit piece of evidence concerning this

[7] Ibid., 149:58–63.
[8] Saint Irenaeus, *Adversus hæreses*, 3, 3, 2.

tradition is provided by two Popes: Siricius and Innocent I.

Bishop Himerius of Tarragona had addressed some specific questions to Pope Damasus, but it was his successor, Pope Siricius, who actually responded to them. To a question concerning the obligation of continence for major clerics, the Pope responded in the letter *Directa* of 385.[9] He stated that those many priests and deacons who, even after ordination, have children act against an irrevocable law which has bound major clerics from the beginning of the Church. Their appeal to the Old Testament, in which the priests and Levites could use their marriage rights outside the time of their service in the Temple, had been refuted by the New Testament, in which the major clerics had to offer daily their sacred service. Thus from the day of their ordination they were obliged to live in perpetual continence.

A second letter of the same Pontiff concerning clerical continence has been mentioned above, to wit, that sent to the African bishops in 386 which communicated the deliberations of the Roman Synod. This letter is particularly revealing for our study. In the first place, the Pope makes the point that the Synod did not deal with new obligations but rather with aspects of faith and discipline which had been neglected. They

[9] Decretal *Directa*. P. Jaffé, *Regesta pontificum Romanorum* (Leipzig, 1851; 2d ed., 1881–88 in 2 vol.; photostatic reprint: Graz, 1956), no. 255. *Patrologia Latina* (PL), ed. by J. P. Migne, 13:1131–47.

had to be observed again because they concerned regulations of the apostolic fathers. As the words of Scripture made clear: "Stand firm, and keep the traditions that we taught you whether by word of mouth or by letter" (2 Th 2:15).

The Roman Council was therefore well aware that oral traditions were also binding. Further, taking into account that they were under divine judgment, all the Catholic bishops there assembled were then held to observe nine specific regulations.

The ninth was widely expounded: priests and Levites must not have sexual relations with their spouses as they were daily occupied in their priestly ministry. Saint Paul had written to the Corinthians stating that they should abstain in order to dedicate themselves to prayer. If continence was imposed on the laity in order that their prayers might be granted, how much greater the obligation on priests, who in a state of purity had to be ready at any moment to offer the sacrifice and administer baptism. After some further considerations concerning ascetic matters, the eighty bishops present rejected for the first time something which is also heard today, to wit, the objection that argues for the continued use of marriage based on the words of Saint Paul according to which a candidate for ordination must be married only once. According to the bishops, this did not mean that he could continue to live with the desire to beget children: rather the injunction of Saint Paul in fact refers to future continence. Officially for the first time we hear something that will constantly be re-iterated; namely, that after the ordination of someone previously married, there is no guarantee that the absti-nence required will be practiced if the person needed to remarry.

The letter concludes with a ringing exhortation to obey these rules which are supported by tradition.[10]

The next Roman Pontiff particularly concerned with clerical continence was Innocent I (401–417). A letter which at first was attributed to Damasus and then to Siricius is in fact probably his. As a result of a query put to him by bishops from Gaul, a series of prac-tical questions was examined in a Roman Synod, and its conclusions were communicated in the letter *Domi-nus inter* (at the beginning of the fifth century). The third of the sixteen questions concerned the "Chastity and Purity of Priests". In the introduction, the Pope noted that "in various Churches many bishops [have let themselves be led] by a most human presumption and hastened to alter the tradition of the Fathers with great prejudice to the reputation attached to their dig-nity; they have thus fallen into the darkness of heresy while taking pleasure in the plaudits of men instead of endeavoring to receive their reward from God." The questioner, who was moved, not by simple curiosity, but rather by a desire for sound faith, based on the

---

[10] Decretal *Cum in unum* (*Diversa quamvis*), a. 386. Jaffé, 258. Bruns, 1:152–55; *Corpus Christianorum* 149:59–63.

authority of the Apostolic See, wanted a clear idea of both laws and traditions. The reply was framed in simple language, and the content was abundantly clear, so that he was in a position to correct the confusion and divergent opinions that were the result of human arrogance.

To the third question, the following response was given: "In the first place it has been decided with respect to bishops, priests and deacons who are obliged to participate in the divine sacrifices, through whose hands the grace of baptism is communicated and the Body of Christ is offered, that they are bound not only by us but by the divine Scriptures to chastity; to which effect the fathers have also enjoined corporal continence." The exhortation is justified in the first place by Sacred Scripture—a fact which is worth underlining even today. It concludes by stating that, even on the basis of the veneration demanded by religion, one should not entrust the mystery of God to the disobedient.[11]

Three further letters of the same Pontiff repeat the ideas of his predecessor with which he fully agrees: the letter to Victricius of Rouen, February 15, 404; that addressed to Exuperius of Toulouse, February 20, 405; and finally that to the bishops Maximus and Severus of Calabria of whose date we are uncertain.[12]

It is important to note the requirement that sanctions

[11] Bruns, 2:274: can. 3 = 276–77.

[12] Jaffé, 286. PL 20, 465–77; Jaffé, 2d ed., 293. PL 20, 495–98, and

are always to be imposed against the unrepentant: they are to be removed from the clerical ministry.

Successive Pontiffs continued to dedicate themselves to emphasizing the need for a strict observance of traditional clerical continence. In this context it is sufficient to refer to the evidence of two of the more important representatives of this and the following century.

In 456 Leo the Great wrote to bishop Rusticus of Narbonne: "The law of continence is the same for the ministers of the altar, for the bishops and for the priests; when they were [still] laymen or lectors, they could freely take a wife and have children. But once they have reached the ranks mentioned above, what had been permitted is no longer so. This is why, in order for [their] union to change from carnal to spiritual, they must, without sending away their wives, live with them as if they did not have them, so that conjugal love be safeguarded and nuptial activity be ended."[13]

This letter underlines another important aspect of the commitment of clerics to continence which had also been mentioned in previous legislation. Namely, that the spouses of those major clerics who had been ordained had to be supported by the Church, either

---

Conc. Agathense, a. 506, no. 9, in: *Corpus Christianorum* 148:196–99; Jaffé, 315. PL 20, 605.

[13] Jaffé, 544. PL 54, 1199.

by entering a convent or by living in a community of women specifically established by the Church. Further cohabitation with the husband who was now held to continence was generally not tolerated because of the danger of not remaining faithful to the obligation that had been undertaken. Cohabitation was only permitted in those cases in which this danger had been excluded.

It should be noted that Pope Leo had already extended the obligation of continence after ordination to subdeacons—an issue that was not entirely clear, given the doubts as to whether or not the subdiaconate was part of the major orders.[14]

Gregory the Great (590–604) made it clear, at least indirectly, in his letters that clerical continence was generally observed in the Western Church. He stated simply that even the ordination to the subdiaconate definitively carried with it the obligation to perfect continence. Further, he repeatedly dedicated himself to ensuring that any common life between major clerics and women which was not authorized was to be prohibited and prevented at all costs. Given that spouses did not normally belong to the category of those authorized, he thereby provided a perceptive interpretation of the relevant canon 3 of the Council of Nicaea.[15]

---

[14] Letter to Anastasius of Thessalonica of the year 446: Jaffé, 411. PL 54, 666.

[15] On the numerous texts of Gregory the Great, cf. Christian Cochini, S.J, *Origines apostoliques du célibat*, Le Sycomore (Paris: Lethielleux, 1981); English trans.: *Apostolic Origins of Priestly Celibacy* (San

From what has so far been said, one can make a very important initial assertion: in the Western Church, that is, in Europe and in the regions of Africa that were part of the patriarchate of Rome, the unity of faith and discipline was and always remained alive and active. This was particularly reflected in the unbroken communion that existed between the various regional Churches. Hence representatives from particular regions were recognized at other regional councils. The priest Eutyches was present as the representative of Carthage at the Council of Elvira, and we find bishops from Spain present at the Council of Carthage of 418 which dealt with the Pelagian question.[16]

The conciliar acts of the period underline and confirm this awareness of genuine unity and essential uniformity.[17] It was, however, made real and translated into practice by the principle of unity, that is, the Roman primacy, which became more active and significant at the end of the period of persecution. Such activity and concern showed themselves especially through its involvement in those essential questions of the faith

---

Francisco: Ignatius Press, 1990), 371–82; for example: "subdiaconi . . . qui iam uxoribus fuerant copulati, unum ex duobus eligerent: id est a suis uxoribus abstinerent aut certe nulla ratione ministrare præsumerent" (*Monumenta Germaniæ Historica*, Epistolæ 4, 36 = PL 77, 710).

[16] Bruns, 2:2. *Corpus Christianorum* 149:69.

[17] For example, Conc. Tol. I (a. 398): Bruns, 1:203; Conc. Romanum a. 348: Bruns, 2:278 (can. 6).

which were relevant to the whole universal Church. This is particularly reflected by its concern with those various disciplinary matters in the regions covered by the Roman patriarchate.

We find a particularly significant proof of this unity of discipline in the question of the continence of the major clergy. Alongside conciliar praxis, which had initially played an important role through various enactments and declarations, we find a growing awareness of and constant concern for the question of clerical continence on the part of the Roman Pontiffs, beginning with Pope Siricius. In fact it was due to this constant pastoral care and concern on the part of the Popes that clerical celibacy, correctly understood in terms of its origins and ancient tradition, was actually preserved despite the regular and ongoing difficulties associated with it. A further proof of this is also provided by the history of celibacy-continence in the Oriental Church.

Nonetheless, before turning to consider the Eastern Churches, we still need to consider further aspects of the development of celibacy in the Western Church.

The most important evidence concerning the faith and tradition in the first centuries of the Church's history comes from the Church Fathers and ecclesiastical writers. In the first place, it is useful to consider what Saint Ambrose had to say on the question of clerical continence. Ambrose, who had been Consul of Emilia and Liguria, was elected bishop of Milan and quickly became one of the most important figures in the West-

ern Church. This pastor had very clear ideas concerning our theme and in the light of his former civil re-
sponsibilities was particularly sensitive to juridical obligations. He clearly stated that even ministers of the
altar who had been married before ordination could
not continue the use of marriage after ordination, even
if in remote areas such an obligation was not always
observed as it should be. In comparison with the Old
Testament, we are dealing with a new commandment
of the New Covenant, since priests of the New Testament are obliged to constant prayer and a holy ministry.[18]

We know that Saint Jerome was well acquainted
with the tradition of both the West and the East—the
latter, indeed, from personal experience. In his refu-
tation of Jovinian (393), he stated, without implying
there was any distinction between East and West, that
the Apostle Saint Paul in the well-known passage of his
letter to Titus, had said that a married candidate to sacred orders must have contracted marriage only once,
must have properly educated his children, but could
not have further children. He was obliged to dedicate himself constantly to prayer and to divine service
and not only during certain periods as was the case in
the Old Testament. Thus he could remark: "si semper
orandum et ergo semper carendum matrimonio."[19]

[18] *De officiis ministrorum* 1, 50: PL 16, 103–5. Cf. also the letter to
the Church of Vercelli = 63, 62ff. = PL 16, 1257.

[19] Ibid., 1, 34 = PL 23, 257.

In his treatise *Adversus Vigilantium* (406), Saint Jerome reiterated the obligation that ministers of the altar had to live in permanent continence. In line with this, he stated that this was the praxis of the Eastern Church, of the Egyptian Church and of the Apostolic See, and that in these churches only those clerics were accepted who were celibate and continent or, if married, had first renounced the matrimonial life.[20] Already in his *Apologeticum ad Pammachium*, he had stated that the apostles were "vel virgines vel post nuptias continentes"[21]; and "presbyteri, episcopi, diaconi aut virgines eliguntur, aut vidui aut certo post sacerdotium in æternum pudici."[22]

Saint Augustine, bishop of Hippo from 395/96, was not only conscious of the general obligation to continence for major clerics but had also participated at the Council of Carthage in which the obligation had been repeatedly affirmed and traced back to the apostles and to a constant tradition. There is no indication that he disagreed with this view. In his treatise *De coniugiis adulterinis*, he asserted that even married men, who unexpectedly and therefore to an extent against their will were called to enter the ranks of the major clergy and were then ordained, were obliged to conti-

[20] PL 23, 340-41: "Aut virgines, aut continentes aut si uxores habuerint mariti esse desistunt."

[21] Ep. 49, 21 = *Corpus scriptorum ecclesiasticorum latinorum* (CSEL) 54, 386ff.

[22] PL 22, 510.

nence. In this they became an example to those laymen
who had to live separated from their wives and who
therefore were more liable to be tempted to commit
adultery.[23]

In our discussion above, we have referred to the
ideas on clerical continence of Gregory the Great, the
fourth great Father of the Western Church.

From what has been analyzed to this point concerning the disciplinary praxis of the Western Church, we
can make the following assertion: that the three higher
grades of the clerical ministry were clearly obliged
to clerical continence, that such an obligation can be
traced to the very beginnings of the Church and that
it had been handed down as part of the oral tradition.
After the period of the persecution of the Church and
especially due to the increasing numbers converting,
which also meant an increase in the number of ordinations, we find infractions against this difficult obligation. Against such infractions, both councils and Popes
insisted with ever-increasing determination on the obligation to continence by means of written laws or regulations.

These particular regulations and provisions appear
to be, not innovations, but rather part of an unbroken
normative tradition. Even before it had become fixed
in written laws, a genuinely binding obligation had
been handed on by the oral tradition of the Church.

---

[23] 2, 22 = CSEL 41, 409 and PL 40, 486.

In this way the disciplinary praxis reflects and conforms to the rules of a sound historical-juridical methodology. To suggest the contrary would not only fly in the face of a clear and precise scientific method but also reject as false the clear and unanimous evidence that has been studied and analyzed.

Given what we know of the clear praxis of the early Church, we are now in a position to trace the development of ecclesiastical celibacy in the following centuries. We will turn in the first place to the Western Church.

There can be no doubt that in the following centuries many sacred ministers were chosen from married men. This is clearly demonstrated by the numerous councils in Spain and Gaul in which the obligation to continence for such ministers is repeatedly and constantly insisted upon.[24] We also find that the sanctions imposed were milder. Thus, for example, at the Council of Tours (461) the sanction imposed on those who continued to violate the law was not excommunication for life but exclusion from ecclesiastical service.[25]

---

[24] For the respective councils see: Cochini, 295–308; 355–79; 420–31 (Spain and Gaul). Alfons M. Stickler, "Tratti salienti nella storia del celibato", in: *Sacra Doctrina* 60 (1970): 592–93; "L'Évolution de la discipline du célibat dans l'Église en Occident de la fin de l'âge patristique au concile de Trente", in: J. Coppens, ed., *Sacerdoce et célibat*, Bibliotheca Ephemeridum Theol. Lovanien 28 (1971), 373–94 passim.

[25] Stickler, "Tratti salienti", 593.

On the other hand, we find the Church more and more choosing celibate candidates for major orders, which meant a reduction in the numbers chosen from those who were married. Experience had taught that married candidates, as a result of human weakness, were constantly in danger of failing to fulfill the obligations they had assumed.

Another regulation which was constantly reiterated and renewed was the prohibition against any cohabitation between higher clerics and women. There was always doubt as to whether or not they could actually observe continence if they lived under the same roof.

Of considerable significance for a complete understanding of the discipline of celibacy in medieval Europe are the relevant regulations of the Celtic Churches. The Penitential Books, which faithfully reflected the actual life and discipline practiced in these particular Churches, asserted the same obligation to continence for those higher clerics who had been previously married. Those who after ordination continued the use of marriage with their wife were considered guilty of adultery and punished accordingly.[26] That these serious obligations were insisted upon and substantially observed in the Celtic Churches, of whose rude customs we find a lively witness in the Penitential Books, is the best proof that celibacy was founded on an old and venerable tradition which no one doubted.

[26] Ibid., 594, with no. 21. Id., "L'Évolution", 379–83.

Alongside the general dangers that constantly threatened the living out of clerical continence, a study of the history of the Church confirms that under specific circumstances and in particular regions extraordinary dangers emerged. These situations provoked the authorities of the Church to action. Difficulties of this type were often a result of widespread heresies. An example of this type of phenomenon can be seen in the Arianism which continued among the Visigoths of the Iberian peninsula even after their conversion to Catholicism. In this context, the Councils of both Toledo III (569) and Zaragoza II (592) included explicit norms for those clerics who returned to the faith from Arianism.[27]

One of the most significant crises that had a profound effect on the question of clerical continence in all regions of the Western Church arose from the disorders which necessitated the Gregorian Reform of the eleventh and twelfth centuries. Specifically the problem involved those parts of Europe in which, to varying degrees, the so-called ecclesiastical benefice system had penetrated. During this period the benefice system dominated the public life and consequently also the private life of the Church and the ecclesiastical community in general.

The patrimonial goods of the ecclesiastical benefice, linked to both the higher and lower offices in the

---

[27] Stickler, "Tratti salienti", 592ff.

Church, meant that the holder of the benefice, and therefore of the office as well, was generally independent. Economically independent and often also professionally independent, the holder of the office to which the benefice was attached could be removed only with great difficulty. The conferral of the benefice-office, which was often effected through authorized laymen who had that right, meant that ecclesiastical offices were often filled by candidates—bishops, abbots and priests—who were often unprepared or frankly unworthy. The concession and assignment of ecclesiastical offices by powerful laymen who in these affairs were concerned more with their own secular and worldly interests than with the spiritual and religious ones of the Church resulted in the two fundamental evils of ecclesiastical life of that period: simony, or the buying of ecclesiastical offices, and Nicolaitism, that is, the widespread violation of clerical celibacy.

After the failure of regional reforms, the Popes began to concern themselves with this dangerous situation in the European Church. They succeeded, especially with the decisive action of Gregory VII, to meet this grave risk which had involved all the highest grades of the Church hierarchy.[28]

Thus this threat to ecclesiastical order in fact became a stimulus for the reestablishment of the ancient disci-

[28] Stickler, "L'Évolution", 394–408 and id., "I presupposti storico-giuridici della riforma gregoriana e dell'azione personale di Gregorio VII", in: *Studi Gregoriani* 13 (Rome, 1989): 1–15.

pline of continence. In order effectively to overcome the problem, an effort was made to choose better candidates who would also be formed more effectively. Further, as part of the effort to return to the general observance of the obligation to continence, the number of married men accepted for ordination was gradually limited.

Another important consequence of this reform was the regulation, solemnly decided at the Second Lateran Council (1139), that marriage contracted by higher clerics (and also by those consecrated by religious vows) would be considered not only as gravely illicit but also invalid.[29] This led to a misunderstanding which is widespread even today—namely, the view that celibacy for higher clerics was introduced only at the Second Lateran Council. In reality, the Council declared invalid something that had in fact always been prohibited. In other words, this new sanction actually confirmed an obligation that had in fact existed for many centuries.

At virtually the same time as the decision of the Second Lateran Council, the Church also began to witness the beginnings of the science of canon law. Around 1142 the Camaldolese monk Gratian composed at Bologna his *Concordia discordantium canonum*, later known simply as the *Decretum Gratiani* (the *Decre-*

---

[29] Cf. can. 7, Conc. Lateranen. II, in: *Conciliorum Œcumenicorum Decreta* (Freiburg im Breisgau: Herder, 1962), 174.

tum of Gratian), in which he collected all the juridical material of the Church's first millennium and sought to bring order to these various norms. In parallel with the school of Roman law, with Gratian we can see the beginning of a school of canon law which developed in a particular way through the studies of the glossators, the interpreters of the collections of ecclesiastical law.[30]

The *Decretum* of Gratian naturally dealt with the question and obligation of clerical continence, specifically in Distinctions 26–34 and 81–84. Similar discussions on this topic can be found in the other parts of the *Corpus Iuris Canonici*, which was gradually being formed as further laws were promulgated. In order to understand correctly the various explanations that canonists gave to these laws, we need to take into account that they had not developed a theory for the study of legal history. This first came to light as a result of the work of the humanistic juridical schools of the sixteenth century. We should not therefore be surprised if the glossators—of either the Roman or canon law—did not have the necessary critical approach for the study of the sources and the texts.

This is of particular importance for our theme, since in Gratian we are immediately confronted by the fact that, in treating the question of celibacy, he uncriti-

---

[30] Cf. my *Historia Fontium Iuris Canonici Latini* I (Turin, 1950; reprinted: Rome, 1985), 197ff.

cally accepted as true both the story of the interven-
tion of Paphnutius at the Council of Nicaea as well
as canon 13 of the Second Council of Trullo of 691.
From this he accepted uncritically the different praxis
concerning celibacy as found in the Eastern and Western Churches. While he did not accept this as binding for the Latin Church, it did nevertheless provide
both him and the classic school of canon law with the
principal reason for the different obligation with respect to celibacy that was found in the Eastern Church.
We will consider this difference when we discuss the
history of celibacy in the Eastern Church. As a result of this lack of care in approaching the texts criti-
cally, doubts concerning the falsification of texts which
had been voiced in the West, particularly by Gregory
VII, Bernold of Constance and other reformers, did
not have a decisive impact on canonical studies. The
classic canon law recognized the deliberations of the
Second Trullan Council as fully valid for the Eastern
Church. It was at this Council, which took place even
before the formal schism between East and West, that
the different discipline on celibacy was established for
the Byzantine Church and those who were later to be
dependent on it.

On the other hand, the medieval canonists had no
doubt that higher clerics in the Western Church were
obliged to continence. They were well aware of the
early documents: texts from universal and Eastern and
Western councils, especially of the African councils

(Gratian, however, does not seem to have known canon
33 of Elvira); letters of the Roman Pontiffs and the
writings of the Fathers. All the canonists agree that
the prohibition against marriage for the higher clergy
can be traced back to the apostles and their example
but, in part, also to their command. The prohibition
on the use of marriage contracted before ordination is
attributed by some to the apostles, by others to later
legislative norms, above all to the Roman Pontiffs beginning with Pope Siricius. In seeking to explain the
reasons for such a prohibition, they are at times con-
tradictory. Some referred to a *votum*, either *expressum*
or *tacitum*, or *ordini adnexum, solemnizatum*, that is, annexed to the order or solemnized by legitimate authority. Faced with the difficulty that no one could impose
a *votum* on another, they sought to find the solution
in the assertion that it was not imposed on the person
but on the office to which the condition was annexed.
The canonists had no doubt that the Church could do
this.

A point of view that had particular merit suggested
that by means of the law this obligation could be united
to sacred orders, especially if sanctioned by the Pope.
They argued that, from the very beginning of the
Church, this had actually been imposed on bishops,
priests and deacons by both councils and Popes. For
subdeacons, this was first definitively decided by Pope
Gregory I. Nevertheless, the medieval canonists had
no doubt that this obligation was binding from the

moment of its introduction. It is of some interest to note the fact that some glossators explicitly refer to the purely customary norms as being the source of the obligation of clerical continence. These customary norms were already in existence prior to their being fixed in a specific legislative form, and it was pointed out that a dispensation from an obligation arising from a vow was not possible even for the Pope. Granted this, many held the theory that the Pope could dispense from a general law. However, a good number of the medieval canonists were of the opinion that such a dispensation could be given only in individual cases. It could not be given for all, as that would be equivalent to the abolition of an obligation that would militate against the *status ecclesiæ*, something which was not possible even for the Pope.[31]

At this point it would be useful to consider some of the more important texts of Raymund of Peñafort, which will provide a summary of the thought of the glossators on the question of celibacy. As one of the most important glossators and entrusted with the compilation of the *Liber Extra* by Gregory IX, Raymund of Peñafort is rightly held as truly representative of the

[31] Cf. Filippo Liotta, *La Continenza dei Chierici nel pensiero canonistico classico (da Graziano a Gregorio IX)*, Quaderni di Studi Senesi 24 (Milan: Giuffrè, 1971), above all 373–87. Chapter IV will deal with the reasons for this development, while the discussion on the discipline, content and evolution in the Eastern Church will be studied in Chapter III.

science of canon law in a period of significant development.

In commenting on the origin and content of the obligation to continence of men married before ordination, he remarks: "The bishops, priests and deacons must observe continence also with their wives. As is stated by some, the apostles have taught this with their example and also with their directives according to which the phrase, 'They have taught', (Dist. 84, can. 3) can be interpreted in various ways. That was later renewed at the Council of Carthage, as in the cited norm *cum in præterito*, and also by Pope Siricius."[32] After having summarized the other explanations, Raymund then looks at the reasons for the introduction of such an obligation: "The reason is twofold: sacerdotal purity, in order that they may obtain in all sincerity that which with their prayers they ask from God (Dist. 84, c. 3 and dict. p. c. 1, Dist. 31); the second reason is that they may pray unhindered (1 Cor 7:5) and exercise their office. They cannot do both things together: that is, to serve their wife and the Church."[33]

This demanding commitment, which involves a life of constant sacrifice, can only be lived out if it is nourished by a living faith, since human weakness is a constant reminder of its practical implications. It is only through a faith that is constantly and con-

[32] Liotta, 374.

[33] Liotta, 386f. For additional reasons found in the glossators, see Chapter IV. Cf. also Stickler, "L'Évolution", 408–27.

sciously sustained that the supernatural reasons under-
lying the commitment can be truly understood. When
this faith grows weak, the determination to persevere
fades; when faith dies, so does continence.

A constant proof of this truth is to be found in the
various heretical and schismatic movements that have
arisen in the Church. One of the first institutions to
be attacked is clerical continence. Therefore we should
not be surprised that one of the first things that was
rejected by the heretical movements that broke away
from the unity of the Catholic Church in the sixteenth
century—Lutherans, Calvinists, Zwinglians, Anglicans
—was in fact clerical celibacy. The Council of Trent in
its determination to reform the Church and to reestablish the true faith and sound discipline also had to respond to attacks which had been made against clerical
continence.

The history of the Council is marked by attempts
to modify the law on celibacy. We know that in a
particular way, emperors, kings and princes, as well as
representatives of the Church herself, were involved in
an attempt at securing a relaxation of or a dispensation
from the obligation to celibacy. They had a positive
objective; namely, to win back those ministers who had
left the Catholic Church. Nonetheless, a commission
established by the Roman Pontiffs to treat of this question came to the conclusion, on the basis of the ancient
tradition, that the commitment to celibacy was to be
maintained without compromise. The Church could

not reject an obligation which had been valid from
the very beginning and which had been constantly repeated and enforced throughout the centuries.[34]

For pastoral reasons, special authorization was given
to Germany and England. After they had renounced
every use of marriage, apostate priests could be ab-
solved and reintegrated into their ministry in the Catholic Church. If they refused, the invalidity of their
matrimony could be sanated, but they were always
excluded from any priestly ministry.[35]

It should also be noted that the Fathers of the Council of Trent not only renewed all the particular obligations relative to celibacy, but they also refused to
declare that the law of celibacy of the Latin Church
was a purely ecclesiastical law,[36] as they also refused

[34] The Fathers here referred expressly to the provisions of the Councils of Carthage which have been discussed above. We have here a
proof of the extent to which the ancient tradition was still alive among
the Fathers. Cf. "Concilium Tridentinum", in: *Goerresiana* 9, pars. 6,
425–70.

[35] Cf. Stickler, "L'Évolution", 427–39, and A. Franzen, *Zölibat und
Priesterehe in der katholischen Reform des 16. Jahrhunderts* (Münster, 1969;
2d ed., 1970), 64–88; also, Martin Boelens, "Die Klerikerehe in der
kirchlichen Gesetzgebung zwischen den Konzilien Basel und Trient",
in: *Archiv für katholisches Kirchenrecht* 138 (1969): 75–81.

[36] In the above-mentioned theological commission, the opinions on
the apostolic or ecclesiastical origins were divided. Given the tradition, the question was not decided. Cf. also on this: Franzen, 84, no.
99. Nonetheless, the remarks of one of the supporters of the apostolic
origins is worth noting: Franciscus Orantes remarks apropos: "Apostoli statuerunt atque præceperunt, ut sacerdotes uxores non ducerent.

to include Mary among those who were born with original sin.

But the act of the Council of Trent which had the greatest impact on the preservation and promotion of clerical celibacy is to be found in the decision taken in session XXIII, canon 18. This obliged all dioceses to establish seminaries for the education of priests. It was in these seminaries that young men chosen for the priesthood were consequently formed and strengthened for their ministry.[37]

This farsighted decision was gradually implemented throughout the Church. It meant that many unmarried candidates were formed for the higher grades of the ministry and, in consequence, married men were in general not ordained. Many Fathers at the Council had in fact expressed this wish.[38]

Traditio autem apostolica universaliter i.e. consensu totius Ecclesiæ recepta et perpetuo servata ius divinum dicitur" (*Goerresiana* 9, pars. 6, 440). The citation is found in Roman Cholij, "De lege cœlibatus sacerdotalis nova investigationis elementa", in: *Periodica de re morali, canonica, liturgica* 78 (1989): 184.

[37] *Conciliorum Œcumenicorum Decreta*, 726-29.

[38] On this, see the comments of the council theologian Desiderius de S. Martino: "Cum autem quæritur, an, ubi est penuria sacerdotum, debeant admitti mariti ad sacerdotium, respondeo id non expedire ut fiat, cum id numquam in ecclesia catholica factum fuerit. Cum autem cum voluntate uxorum fieret [something that in reality has always been the case] posset, sed tamen ut ipsi et uxores etiam manerent cœlibes" (*Goerresiana* 9, pars. 6, 441). Cited in Cholij, "De lege cœlibatus", 172, nos. 33 and 185.

Henceforth the concept of celibacy, which could mean either the obligation of complete continence in regard to the use of a marriage contracted before ordination or the prohibition of a future marriage, was now restricted to this latter understanding. This is how it is generally understood in the mind of today's faithful, that is, that clerical celibacy is commonly understood only as a prohibition against marrying.

Even during subsequent difficult periods in her history, the Church has always been resolute in defending and preserving her tradition of celibacy. A clear proof of this can be seen in the response to the situation of the French Church during the Revolution at the end of the eighteenth and beginning of the nineteenth century. The priests who were married during the Revolution had to decide either to renounce a civil marriage invalidly contracted or to allow the Church to sanate the invalidity. In the first case, they could be readmitted to the sacred ministry; in the second, they were permanently excluded from this ministry. This should come as no surprise if we recall that such an approach had already been adopted by the first written law concerning this matter at the Council of Elvira.

The Church has constantly opposed all other attempts that have been made to abolish clerical celibacy. Illustrative of this resolve were the efforts made in Baden-Würtemberg under Gregory XVI[39] or against

---

[39] *Mirari vos*, August 15, 1832, in: *Acta Gregorii XVI*, 1:171.

the Jednota movement in Bohemia under Benedict XV.[40]

It is again significant that the Old Catholics immediately abolished celibacy after the First Vatican Council. Nevertheless, the Church has continually opposed any attempts to alter the discipline and tradition of celibacy. After Vatican II there have been a number of efforts to change the discipline: to wit, on the one hand, the attempt to ordain married men (*viri probati*), without demanding the renunciation of the use of marriage and, on the other, the attempt to permit priests to marry. Nevertheless, it is of considerable importance to note the Church's constant opposition to such attempts.

[40] Consistorial Allocution, December 16, 1920, in: AAS 12 (1920): 587.

III

THE PRACTICE
IN THE EASTERN CHURCH

T HE LATIN CHURCH has often been criticized for
having developed a stricter and more severe discipline of clerical celibacy than the more open and lib-
eral attitude that is generally considered to have been
the situation at the beginning of the Church. Support
for this view is made by appealing to the praxis of the
Eastern Church, which is supposed to have preserved
the original general discipline of the primitive Church.
The argument continues that the Latin Church should
return to the original discipline, especially as celibacy
now seems to be a particularly harsh burden in the
present pastoral situation of the universal Church.

The response to this particular assertion and to various other similar proposals clearly depends on whether
or not the claims made for the primitive Church are
in fact valid. Certainly the results of our historical ex-
amination of the actual praxis of celibacy in the West
suggest a certain doubt concerning the claims made
for the early Church. It is therefore necessary to be

quite clear about the actual development of celibacy in the Eastern Church. It is to this end that the present chapter is devoted.

In his defense of the apostolic origins of celibacy, Gustav Bickell appealed above all to the evidence of the East. We clearly cannot examine all the existing evidence relative to the history of celibacy in the East.[1] Nevertheless, on the basis of past scholarship and what will be discussed in this chapter, a secure and reasonable idea of the real situation in the Eastern Church can be reached.

An important first witness is Bishop Epiphanius of Salamis, later elevated to the episcopal see of Constantia (ancient Salamis) in Cyprus (315–403). He was well known as an expert defender of orthodoxy and of the tradition of the Church, which he would have known well during his long life of eighty-six years, spanning almost all of the fourth century. Even if in some aspects, especially in his views on Origen, Epiphanius demonstrated a somewhat misdirected enthusiasm, he nevertheless remains a credible witness to the realities and conditions of his time, especially with respect to the discipline of the Church.

Concerning the question of the continence of the higher clergy, he provides us with a typical account of

---

[1] For further details, see Gustav Bickell, op. cit., and Roman Cholij, *Clerical Celibacy in East and West* (Leominster: Fowler Wright Books), 69–105.

the actual situation. In his principal work, the *Panarion*, written in the second half of the fourth century, he states that the God of the world has shown the charism of the new priesthood, either through men who have renounced the use of their sole marriage contracted before ordination or through those who have always lived as virgins. That, he says, is the norm which was established by the apostles in both wisdom and holiness.[2]

Of even more importance is the assertion that he makes in his "*Expositio fidei*", the preface to his principal work. The Church, he says, admits to the episcopal and priestly ministry and also to the diaconal ministry only those who renounce, in continence, their own spouses or who have become widowers. He continues that at least here one can see that the provisions of the Church are faithfully observed. However, it can also be asserted that, in various places, priests, deacons and subdeacons continue to have children. He claims nonetheless that this does not correspond to the actual norm but is rather a consequence of human weakness which always takes the easier path. He further explains that priests are chosen above all from those who are celibate or monks. If sufficient candidates cannot be found from this group, then they will also be chosen either from the married, who, however, have to

---

[2] *Patrologia Græca* (PG) 41, 868, 1024, or *Die griechischen christlichen Schriftsteller der ersten drei Jahrhunderte* (GCS) 31 (1921): 219f.

renounce the use of marriage, or from among those who, after a sole marriage, have become widowers.[3]

These assertions made by an individual who knew many languages and who had an intimate knowledge of the Church during a period in which she was already divided by many doctrines, are a reliable and significant testimony to the common norms as well as to the actual situation concerning the praxis of celibacy in the Eastern Church.

A second witness to the actual situation has already been noted. Saint Jerome was ordained priest in Asia Minor around 379 and then, in the space of six years, became acquainted with Church officials, communities of monks as well as the doctrines and the discipline of the East. After having lived for three years at Rome, he returned through Egypt to Palestine, where he remained until his death around 420. He always remained in close contact with the life of the whole Church, in a particular way due to his friendship with many important contemporary individuals in both East and West and also as a result of his extensive knowledge of many languages.

Reference has already been made to his comments on clerical continence, and here we want to consider again his work *Adversus Vigilantium*, in which he argued against a priest of southern Gaul who despised celibacy. In this he appealed to the praxis of the Churches of

[3] PG 42, 823ff. or GCS 37 (1933): 522.

the East, of Egypt and of the Apostolic See, affirming that they all accepted only clerics who were virgins and continent or, if married, those who had renounced the use of marriage.[4] Again we have here an important piece of evidence with respect to the official position of the Eastern Church on clerical continence.

A glance at the legislation of the Eastern synods indicates that the regional councils before Nicaea, those of Ancyra and Neocaesarea, and also the one after Nicaea, Gangra, speak of higher clerics who were married, but, apart from some explicit exceptions, they do not provide reliable information on the possible use of marriage after ordination.[5]

Further, in the particular synods of the various schismatic Churches of the East, which were established as a consequence of the christological controversies and in which a divergence from the discipline of continence can be seen, we actually have further evidence of an attitude which was in fact contrary to Orthodoxy.

Nevertheless, given our theme, the council which must concern us more closely is the First Ecumenical Council held in Nicaea in 325.

The particular provision of this first council of the universal Church which concerned clerical celibacy is canon 3, which prohibited bishops, priests, deacons

---

[4] See above, Chapter II, note 20.

[5] See for example Christian Cochini, S.J., *Apostolic Origins of Priestly Celibacy* (San Francisco: Ignatius Press, 1990), 169–78, 201–2, and also Cholij, *Clerical Celibacy in East and West*, 39–40, 75–78, 92–97.

and in general all clerics from furtively introducing women into their homes. The only exception was for the mother, sister or aunt or for others who were above every suspicion.[6] Interestingly the wife does not figure among the women who were permitted to live in the house of the cleric. We may well ask ourselves if this does not indeed reflect the fact that among the Fathers of the Council there was a solid conviction about and understanding of the obligation to continence. This is especially so if we consider the fact that, among those ecclesiastics who were subject to the prohibition against cohabitation, it was the bishop who was listed first. Indeed the Eastern Church has always demanded and continues to demand that a bishop not use the rights of a previously contracted marriage.

Paphnutius, a hermit and bishop of the desert in Egypt, is supposed to have put forward a different position for priests, deacons and subdeacons. He is alleged to have risen during the Council to dissuade the Fathers from sanctioning a general obligation to continence. He suggested that this ought to be left to the decision of particular Churches, and the argument goes that his advice is supposed to have been accepted by the assembly.

The well-known historian of the Church, Eusebius of Caesarea, who was both present at the Council and

---

[6] *Conciliorum Œcumenicorum Decreta* (Freiburg im Breisgau: Herder, 1962), 6. The deacons are not found in the Latin text of this edition.

sympathetic to the Arians, does not make any reference to this episode which does have some importance for the Church. In fact it is some one hundred years after the Council that we hear of this episode for the first time from two Byzantine ecclesiastical writers, Socrates and Sozomen. Socrates claims that his source was a very old man who is supposed to have been present at the Council and who had recounted the episode to him. If one considers that Socrates, born around 380, heard this story when he was still quite young, from someone who in 325 could not have been more than a child and could certainly not be considered a reliable witness to the events of the Council, even the most fundamental critique of the sources would suggest that there are serious doubts as to the authenticity of this story.

Doubts as to the truth of this story were soon raised. As has already been noted, both Pope Gregory VII and Bernold of Constance questioned the truthfulness of the episode. In addition we need to consider the commentary made on this story by Valesius, editor of the works of Socrates and Sozomen, which Migne printed in his *Patrologia Græca*, (vol. 67). Valesius expressly says that the story of Paphnutius is suspect, because, among the Fathers of the Council coming from Egypt, no bishop of that name appears. Further, with respect to the relevant passage of the story by Sozomen, he again repeats that the story of Paphnutius is an invented fable, especially because, among the Fathers who signed the Acts of the Council of Nicaea no one with this name can be found.[7] In the Latin translation of Cassiodorus-Epiphanius (*Historia tripartita*) we find only an extract of sixteen lines from the account of Sozomen concerning this episode.[8]

The German scholar Friedhelm Winkelmann has studied this question recently and has definitively concluded that the episode is an invention. He offers the following reasons. The person of Paphnutius is found only at a much later stage, his name appearing only in later manuscripts of the Acts of the Council, and in those from the fourth century he is known only as a confessor of the faith; it is only later hagiographic legends that begin to consider him a thaumaturge and Father of the Council of Nicaea.[9]

But the most telling argument against the authenticity of this episode seems to be the fact that the Eastern Church itself, which should have had the greatest interest in it, either did not know of it or, because Eastern church leaders were convinced that it was false, did not have a record of it in any official document they used. Neither the polemical writers on clerical celibacy

[7] PG 67, 100–102, with the footnote (Socrates), and 925f., especially footnote 74 (Sozomen).

[8] PG 69, 933.

[9] Friedhelm Winkelmann, "Paphnutios, der Bekenner und Bischof. Probleme der koptischen Literatur", in: *Wissenschaftliche Beiträge der Martin Luther-Universität Halle-Wittenberg*, 1968/1, 145–53. On the whole question, see also Cochini, *Apostolic Origins of Priestly Celibacy*, 197–200.

nor the great commentators of the twelfth century on the *Syntagma canonum adauctum*—the great code of law of the Eastern Church stemming from the Council of Trullo—(Aristenus, Zonaras, Balsamon) made mention of the story of Paphnutius, although it would have been much simpler than resorting to the manipulation of historical texts which were in fact quite well known.

It was only in the fourteenth century that this account appeared in the *Syntagma Alphabeticum* of Matthaeus Blastares, who, however, seemed to have considered it of interest for the East only after its appearance in the *Decretum* of Gratian. In the West, this falsification was accepted uncritically, at least among canonists, who in part based the Eastern Church's particular discipline of celibacy on it.[10] Rather interestingly, the Second Council of Trullo did not refer to Paphnutius in officially establishing that the rule of celibacy would continue to remain in the future.

With this we have arrived at the central point of the history of clerical celibacy in the Byzantine Church and of those Churches associated with it in the Eastern Rite.

Some preliminary reflections will help us to understand this correctly. In our consideration of the development of celibacy in the Church, we have seen that such a demanding commitment, humanly speaking, has

---

[10] On this see Cholij, 88–91.

always had to take into account human weakness. Saint Ambrose of Milan attested to this when he affirmed that the practice, even in the West, did not always correspond to the precept, especially in very remote areas. Epiphanius of Salamis had made the same comment for the East. In the West, the regional councils and the Popes had always intervened to recall individuals to the observance of continence, to support them in every way and thereby to protect the commitment that had been assumed.

To all appearances, this type of care was lacking in the East. On the one hand, this is confirmed by the history of the Eastern regional councils. It is true that one can see the beneficial effects of the common commitment of the universal Church to various questions, particularly expressed in the ecumenical councils held in the first millennium of the Church in the East. But this commitment referred above all to questions of faith and doctrine. Disciplinary problems and those of a practical-pastoral type were left to the assemblies of the particular Churches, not only because they had to take into account the different conditions in the various regions, but also and above all because of the patriarchal organization (Constantinople, Antioch, Alexandria, Jerusalem) of these Churches. This implied a certain autonomy in government, which was exacerbated by the further separation of not a few of these particular Churches as a result of the christological heresies which had disrupted the Churches of the East.

Thus, the East never reached a comprehensive unity on disciplinary questions, even in those areas of general ecclesiastical discipline which were common to them all. Every particular Church promulgated its own norms, which were often as diverse as their differing ideas and needs.

However, the East especially lacked a universally recognized authority which could effectively coordinate the general discipline of the Church and thereby ensure its effective application. This situation is clearly mirrored in the collections of norms of the Eastern Church which contain the prescriptions of the ecumenical councils as well as those of the particular councils of the first centuries. The particular legislation of the following centuries was not included in the common collection, the *Syntagma canonum*. In place of the pontifical prescriptions (decretals), various passages from the writings of the principal Eastern Fathers as well as imperial laws in ecclesiastical matters were adopted. From the particular discipline of the Western Church, the Eastern Churches included in their own collections of ecclesiastical law only that of the African Church. Even though this Church was geographically close to and well known by the Churches of the East, it was actually part of the Roman patriarchate. In fact, the most important and extensive collection of this Church, the *Codex Canonum Ecclesiæ Africanæ*, or the *Codex Apiarii Causæ*, in which the East had actually been involved, was inserted into its *Syntagma*.

The position and influence exercised in the East by the Byzantine emperors (Caesaropapism) in ecclesiastical questions are reflected in the existence of the so-called *Nomocanones*. These collections included ecclesiastical and state laws in ecclesiastical matters, and the emperor took care that the prescriptions were observed at least for the eastern territories of the Church which were subject to him.

From this brief description of the situation in the Eastern Church, one can begin to understand why there was no effective action taken against the inevitable falling away from the observance of obligatory celibacy by the higher clergy. It is true that the East successfully maintained the ancient tradition of complete continence for bishops, including also those who had been married before ordination. In fact many bishops were now chosen from among monks. On the other hand, it was judged that the use of marriage by priests, deacons and subdeacons contracted before ordination could not be arrested and that the obligation of complete continence could not be reestablished. In other words a de facto situation was accepted.

In fact the Theodosian Code (434) held that continence could be safeguarded even if one permitted the spouse to live with the husband after ordination: a love of chastity did not allow her to be turned out of the home, and her comportment before the ordination of the husband would be further proof that she was worthy.[11] On the other hand, the legislation of the Emperor Justinian both in the *Codex* (534) and in the *Novellæ* (535–565) already reflected a different attitude. The prohibition against admitting anyone to sacred orders who had been married more than once as well as against marrying a second time after ordination was upheld. This included all grades beginning with the subdiaconate. On the other hand, cohabitation with one's wife was now allowed for priests, deacons and subdeacons, so that they could continue the use of marriage, but on the condition that this had been celebrated only once and with a virgin.[12]

What then was the legislation of the Eastern Church itself? As already pointed out, a common legislation in disciplinary matters never existed in the East. Since the First Council of Trullo in Constantinople (680/81) had not promulgated disciplinary norms, the Emperor, Justinian II, convoked a second Council in Trullo in the autumn of 691, which was intended finally to bring order to the disciplinary legislation of the Byzantine Church and the necessary updating of and additions to the law. This was effected through the promulgation of 102 canons which were then added to the old *Syntagma*, which thus became the *Syntagma adauctum,* the last Code of the whole Byzantine Church.[13]

[11] Codex Theodosianus 16, 2, 44.

[12] Alfons M. Stickler, "Tratti salienti nella storia del celibato", in *Sacra Doctrina* 60 (1970), no. 50, n. 1.

[13] Alfons M. Stickler, *Historia Fontium Iuris Canonici Latini*, 69–70.

The full discipline concerning celibacy was fixed in a binding form in seven canons (3, 6, 12, 13, 26, 30, 48).

This Second Council of Trullo (Quinisextum) was a council convoked by and bearing the authority of the Byzantine Church. The Western Church has never recognized this council as ecumenical, notwithstanding repeated efforts to have it so recognized. Pope Sergius I (687–701), who came from Syria, refused to recognize it. Only John VIII (872–882), a Roman, recognized those deliberations which were not contrary to the praxis of the Roman Church in force up to that date. Other references to the decisions of Trullo by the Roman Pontiffs can be considered to reflect their respect for the particular law of the Eastern Church.

What are the sources for the decisions at Trullo concerning the discipline of celibacy in the Byzantine Church which continue to be in force even today? In order adequately to respond to this question, it is necessary in the first place to examine the individual provisions.

Canon 3: establishes that all those who after baptism have contracted a second marriage or have lived in concubinage, as also those who have married a widow, a divorcee, a prostitute, a slave or an actress, cannot become bishops, priests or deacons.

Canon 6: decrees that it is not licit for priests and deacons to contract marriage after ordination.

Canon 12: establishes that bishops cannot, after their ordination, cohabit with their wives and therefore can no more have use of their marriage.

Canon 13: decrees that, contrary to the Roman praxis which prohibits the use of marriage, priests, deacons and subdeacons in the Eastern Church can, on the basis of ancient apostolic prescriptions for perfection and right order, live with their spouses and use marriage, except during those times in which they exercise service at the altar and celebrate the sacred mysteries, during which they must remain continent. This latter point had been stated by the Fathers gathered in Carthage:

> The subdeacons, who touch the sacred mysteries, the deacons and the priests too, should abstain from their wives during the periods that are specifically [assigned] to them, . . . thus we also will keep what was taught by the apostles and observed since antiquity, knowing that there is a time for everything, especially for fasting and prayer; it is indeed necessary that those who approach the altar, when they touch holy things, be continent in every respect so that they may obtain in all simplicity what they are asking from God.

If anyone therefore acting against the apostolic canons dares deprive a cleric in sacred orders, that is, a priest, a deacon or a subdeacon, of conjugal relations and the society of his wife, let him be deposed; in the same way, if a priest or a deacon sends away his wife with the excuse of piety, let him be excommunicated, and if he persists, deposed.

Canon 26: decrees that a priest who through ignorance has contracted an illicit marriage must be satisfied with his first state but must abstain from every priestly ministry. Such a marriage must be dissolved, and all communion with this spouse is prohibited.

Canon 30: permits that those who reciprocally consent to live in continence must not live together; that goes also for priests who live in "barbaric" countries (this was understood to apply to priests who lived in the Western Church). This commitment was considered, however, a dispensation which was accorded to such priests because of their weakness and in consideration of the customs of the regions in which they had to live.

Canon 48: decrees that the spouse of the bishop who separates from him on the basis of common consent must enter a monastery after his ordination and be maintained by him.

A number of conclusions can be drawn from these provisions of the Council. The East was well aware of the praxis of celibacy in the West. As in the West, it appealed for its own particular practice to the tradition that derived from the apostles. In the Trullan legislation, which likewise refers to the New Testament, the Byzantine Church agrees with the Latin Church on the following points: there must be only a single marriage contracted before sacred ordination, and it cannot be with a widow or with other women excluded by the law. After ordination, a first or further marriage is not licit. Bishops can no longer live in marriage with their spouse but must live in complete continence, and therefore their wives can no longer live with them. On the other hand, these wives must be maintained or supported by the Church. The East further requires their entry into a monastery.

The substantial difference between the praxis of the Eastern and Western Church concerns only those grades of sacred orders under the bishop. For these, abstinence from the use of marriage is required only during the time of actual service at the altar, which during this period in the East was not daily but normally limited to Sunday or also another day of the week. In fact we are actually dealing here with the particular praxis of the Old Testament. Cohabitation with one's wife and the use of marriage are now not only resolutely defended, but any different approach is punished with severe sanctions. The exception, understandable for priests living in the regions of the Latin Church, is declared as a dispensation. This is granted on the basis of human weakness and also due to the difficulties that are experienced as a result of the particular circumstances in which they live. One of these circumstances is certainly the general practice of continence by the Western clergy.

The Fathers of Trullo II could not find a reason for the difference between the two disciplines in the documents they had before them. They probably did not want to appeal to the Old Testament, because, as has already been indicated, this type of parallel was explicitly rejected in Western thought and above all in the regulations of the Roman Pontiffs in favor of complete continence. It no longer adequately explained the reality of the priest of the New Testament. They were even less inclined to refer to imperial legislation which had already anticipated the ecclesiastical decisions and which reflected the general praxis.

Since at Constantinople the story of Paphnutius was clearly shown to be false, the only course open was to go back to the evidence of early Christianity, which in fact did not come from the Constantinopolitan Church but rather from a Church whose disciplinary texts had even been accepted into the General Code of the Eastern Church. They were the canons of the African Church which expressly dealt with clerical continence and did so by directly calling on the apostles and the ancient tradition of the Church.

Since these canons confirmed for priests, deacons and even subdeacons the very same discipline that applied to bishops—namely, complete continence—the authentic text of the African canons had to be modified. Since very few in the East were really able to verify the genuine Latin of the text, this approach to the problem did not present insuperable difficulties. While it is true that these texts required complete continence for all the higher orders, the Eastern Church limited it to those periods of service at the altar, as was the case in the Old Testament. In order to provide an authoritative basis for this practice of the Eastern Church, reference was made to the apostles and to the ancient Church even in those texts that had been manipulated and modified.

What can we say about this action at Trullo? Without doubt the Eastern Fathers felt themselves authorized to promulgate particular provisions for the Byzantine Church since for some time they had established juridical autonomy in the fields of administration and discipline. In fact it was only in doctrinal questions that they felt themselves bound to the decisions of the universal Church which had been made in ecumenical councils and in which they had also participated. It is understandable that the Fathers were concerned and preoccupied with those particular norms which would have a general effect in their own Church. Clearly this meant that they had to take into account the actual situation of clerical celibacy in their Church. They did not see any possibility of fruitful reform. On the other hand, it is quite another question whether such norms as were adopted could really be permitted, especially concerning the practice of clerical celibacy. The fact is that this question necessarily involved the whole Church, and their new approach was specifically contrary to the praxis of the Western Church under the direction of the Roman Pontiffs. In addition, there is no doubt that the method adopted, namely, a manipulation of the texts which meant changing the actual truth of the matter, had to be rejected.[14]

This attitude and approach to the question of celi-

[14] The text of the canons is found in the series under the direction of P. P. Joannu, *Pontificia Commissione per la Redazione del Codice di Diritto Canonico Orientale*, Fonti, fasc. 9, vol. 1/1, 98–241 (= Concilium Trullanum II) and vol. 1/2, 190–436 (Synod of Carthage, 419), Grottaferrata (Rome) 1962. Canon 13 of the Council in Trullo is found at pp. 140–43, the texts of the African councils, pp. 216–18 and 240–41. Canon 70, which also treats of celibacy, is found at pp. 312–13. The Byzantine collection of the *Pedalion* is missing.

The text of canon 13 as formulated at Trullo is as follows (we will follow the Greek text as we do not know the Latin text at the disposition of the Council Fathers): "Scimus autem quod et qui Carthagine convenerunt ministrorum gravitatis in vita curam gerentes dixerunt: 'ut subdiaconi qui sacra contrectant et diaconi et presbyteri [here the words "sed et episcopi" are omitted from the African text] secundum propria statuta et a consortibus se abstineant." This text is taken from canon 25 of Carthage. The Trullan text continues: "Ut quod apostoli docuerunt et ipsa servavit antiquitas nos quoque custodiamus." This text is from the end of canon 3 of Carthage. Then the text proper of Trullo continues: "Tempus pro omni re decernentes et maxime in ieiunio et oratione; oportet enim eos qui divino altari inserviunt, in sanctorum tractandorum tempore." Again we find the text from canon 3 of Carthage: "Continentes esse in omnibus, ut possint id quod a deo simpliciter petunt, obtinere." Then the text proper of Trullo continues: "Si quis ergo præter apostolicos canones incitatus sit aliquem eorum qui sunt in sacris, presbyterorum, iniquimus, vel diaconorum vel subdiaconorum coniunctione cum legitima uxore et consuetudine privare, deponatur. . . ."

We have here a combination of African texts with those of the Fathers at Trullo. The latter omit any reference in canon 13 to bishops, something found at Carthage. They do take up the reference to both the apostolic and the ancient ecclesiastical tradition, and with this they

bacy by the Trullan Fathers constitute a further not unimportant proof that the tradition of the Catholic Church of the West remains the genuine one. The fact is that it can be traced back to the apostles and is founded on the living consciousness of the entire early Church.

This change of texts which was the basis for the new and definitive obligation concerning celibacy in the Oriental Churches was also the object of subsequent historical reflection. The comments of the canonists of the Byzantine Church, for example, those of Matthaeus Blastares, indicate that from the fourteenth century on they had their doubts as to the accuracy of the references to the African texts on the part of the Fathers of the Second Trullan Council and further that they knew the original authentic text. The modern interpreters of the Trullan provisions on celibacy admit that the references are incorrect but add at the same time that the Council had the authority to change any disciplinary law for the Byzantine Church and to adapt it to the conditions of the time. It was on the basis of this same authority that they were also able to change the original sense of the texts of Carthage in order to make them agree with the opinion and the will of the Council itself.[15]

---

wanted to reestablish for priests and deacons a discipline that had not been observed.

[15] C. Knetes, "Ordination and Matrimony in the Eastern Orthodox

From the sixteenth century, historical studies in the West had already noted the change in the texts effected by the Trullan Council. This was recognized by Caesar Baronius[16] and above all by the editors of the various collections of council texts of whom the principal was Giovanni Domenico Mansi.[17]

Church", in: *Journal of Theological Studies* 11 (1910): 354f., and Cholij, 126f.

[16] Caesar Baronius, *Annales Ecclesiastici*, ed. by Giovanni Domenico Mansi in 38 vols. (Lucca, 1738–1759), to which Severin Binius also refers (Mansi 12:50). Baronius states that canon 13 of Trullo is a falsification of the African text. 1:499: "Adsciscentes insuper iidem [the Eastern bishops at Trullo II] ad suum ipsorum confirmandum conatum aperta mendacia, quasi in concilio quod citant carthaginensi statutum fuerit, ut clerici ab uxoribus abstineant tempore vicis suæ quam insigniter mentiantur, ipsa de hac re sæpius ab Africanis Episcopis sancta decreta testantur. Nam non tantum, quem superius citavimus canon secundus Concilii secundi Carthaginensis ut sacris ordinibus mancipati se abstineant ab uxoribus cavit: sed et tertius canon quintæ synodi Carthaginensis hoc ipsum vehementer iniunxit absque aliqua temporis distinctione . . . ut ex his apertissime illorum appareat impostura, quam ut honesto titulo eadem illa seditiosorum factio validaret, ad convellenda statuta Patrum aucupari conata est ex Sextæ Synodi nomine auctoritatem." Baronius provided another discourse on this question, bringing it to the year 692, nos. 19ff.

Although Baronius is not the only Church historian to have made reference to this falsification—other historians of celibacy have also spoken of it—nonetheless it is only with Cholij that it has been seriously considered in the modern literature on the topic.

[17] Mansi 1:58f. Referring to the apostolic canon 5, Severinus Binius regards all the canons of Trullo II "spurios esse." Mansi 11:921ff., especially 930, which asserts that this Council pertains only to the

It is nonetheless important to underline those traces of the genuine and ancient discipline of celibacy that even today remain in the new discipline established at Trullo. For example, the Church was constantly concerned with the risk to those clerics who lived together with women who were not above every suspicion. This concern is found not only in the whole Western legal tradition but also in canon 3 of the Council of Nicaea, which the Council of Trullo also adopted. It reflects a particular determination on the part of the Church to ensure that the continence and purity of her ministers were safeguarded. It is also of some significance that, even under the new Trullan legislation, the bishops of the Eastern Church were held to that particular discipline of continence which had always been valid for the whole Church. This surely reflects those traces of a tradition that had in fact always bound the three or four higher orders to the discipline of continence.

It is difficult actually to understand why in the Eastern Church the condition that candidates for orders be allowed to have been married only once was still

---

Eastern Church. Mansi 12:47ff.: Binius again remarks, col. 50, that canon 13 is contrary to the apostolic provisions and therefore "non immerito hunc canonem cum quibusdam aliis velut spurium et illegittimum partum catholica ecclesia hactenus semper et adversata." At col. 52, Fronton du Duc (Ducæus), S.J., clearly states: "Vitiosa est igitur Græcorum schismaticorum expositio, quæ vitiosa nititur Latini canonis lectione."

kept. As has already been noted, this only makes sense in view of the commitment to continence after ordination. Even more difficult to understand is the absolute prohibition against any marriage whatsoever after someone had been ordained to the higher orders. This particular rule was maintained even given the fact that the use of marriage was licit for those in the priesthood and the lower orders.

The particular innovations on clerical continence officially introduced by Trullo pose a particular problem. It is difficult to reconcile the New Testament concept of priesthood with the Levitical one of the Old Testament when even in the Eastern Rite the higher clergy are involved in ministry at the altar on a daily basis. If we take into consideration the reasons put forward at Trullo itself, this would mean that priests, deacons and subdeacons would be obliged to return to absolute and total continence as is practiced in the West. This has not been done and has meant that service at the altar and the ministry of the Holy Sacrifice have been separated from the commitment to continence, despite the fact that in the East they have always been considered essentially connected.

In the particular Churches which are united to the Byzantine obedience and which have accepted the Trullan discipline, there has been no change in the praxis of celibacy. Rome has allowed those Eastern communities which in time were united to her to continue in their different tradition of celibacy. On the other hand, requests, after their return, that the Latin praxis of complete continence be followed have not been opposed but positively and favorably accepted. The fact that Rome has recognized a different discipline can be seen as a thoughtful gesture but can scarcely be construed as official approbation of a change in the ancient discipline of continence.[18]

[18] Cf. especially Cholij, all of chap. 4 (106–94).

IV

THE THEOLOGICAL FOUNDATIONS

I N THE CURRENT DISCUSSION on celibacy, the need for a deeper theological understanding of the priesthood is often noted. This would then mean that a genuine and complete theology of celibacy in the Catholic Church could be adequately appreciated and properly understood.[1]

For this reason there is still much work to be done in examining the theological components of the priesthood of the New Testament and, based on this, the significance of clerical celibacy. Both have their roots not only in Sacred Scripture, which is the principal source of Catholic theology, but also in the tradition

---

[1] From the many possible works supporting this affirmation I will choose only one: In a dissertation published in vol. 44 of the *Münsterischen Beiträge zur Theologie* under the title, "Der Streit um den Zölibat im 19 Jahrhundert" (Münster, 1978) (an abstract appeared in *Klerikusblatt, Zeitschrift für Kleriker in Bayern und der Pfalz* 69 [1989]: 254–56), the author, Winfried Leinweber, discussed the arguments for and against celibacy and its connection with the priesthood.

of the Church, which develops and interprets the evidence of the Scriptures.

The priesthood of Jesus Christ is a profound mystery of our faith. To understand it, man must open himself to a supernatural vision and submit human reason to a way of transcendental thinking. In times of a living faith which not only animates and directs the individual believer but permeates and forms the life of the whole believing community, Christ the Priest constitutes the living center of the life of personal and community faith in the consciousness of all.

In times of a loss of the sense of faith, the figure of Christ the Priest increasingly disappears from the consciousness of men and of the world and is no longer at the center of Christian life.

This image of Christ the Priest goes hand in hand with that of the priest of Christ. In times of living faith, the priest has no difficulty recognizing himself in Christ and identifying himself with Him; of seeing and living the essence of his own priesthood in intimate union with that of Christ the Priest; of seeing in Him "the unique source" and "the irreplaceable model" of his own priesthood.

In a climate of rationalism in which all sense of the supernatural is absent from the mind of man, and in a world dominated by secular materialism in which any sense of the spiritual has disappeared, it is becoming even more difficult for the priest to resist a worldly mentality. The supernatural and spiritual identity of his priesthood quickly disappears if he does not consciously force himself to deepen it and to be aware of his intimate union of life with Christ.

Undoubtedly the critical situation through which we are living today means that priests more than ever must have the help of a genuine priestly ascetical and mystical theology. This should take into account the actual present reality, reveal those particular dangers that threaten his priesthood, point out to him the absolute necessity of his priesthood and provide him with those means that the living out of his priestly life requires.

The actual crisis of identity in the Catholic priesthood is clearly reflected in a number of ways: in the renunciation of their ministry by thousands of priests; in the profound secularization on the part of many others who remain in the formal ministry; and finally through the scarcity of vocations, caused by a refusal to respond to the call to priesthood. There is a fundamental need in this situation for a new pastoral approach to priesthood that takes into account concrete conditions and actual needs; which, in a word, responds to the "present context".

It is clear that, based on its full theological tradition, the essence of the Catholic priesthood must once again be revealed. In a similar crisis of the priesthood, the Council of Trent, by means of the definition of the sacrament of orders and of the Eucharist, created the foundations for a mystical theology of the priesthood which reestablished it in the mystical reality of Christ. In response to the theological rationalism of the last century, Matthias Joseph Scheeben made a profound study on the nature of the priesthood. He explained that ordination elevates the man ordained into a supernatural organic union with Christ and that the character which sacred orders imprints forever means that the ordained shares in the priestly function of Christ in a special way.[2]

In recent times, particularly after the Second Vatican Council, the essence of the priesthood has been centered more clearly on the relationship of the priest with Christ. The biblical texts and the theological and canonical doctrines of the past on the union and conformity between Christ and the priest have consequently been deepened and expanded. Therefore, the traditional axiom *sacerdos alter Christus* has been placed in a new theological light.

If Saint Paul could write to the Corinthians (1 Cor 4:1): "This is how one should regard us, as servants of Christ and stewards of the mysteries of God" or (2 Cor 5:20): "So we are ambassadors for Christ; it is as though God were appealing through us, and the appeal that we make in Christ's name is: be reconciled to God", this can be considered as an authentic biblical foundation for the identification of the priest with Christ.

---

[2] *Die Mysterien des Christentums* (Mainz, 1931), 543–46.

In the Second Vatican Council, the same idea was constantly expressed: "The bishops, in a resplendent and visible manner, take the place of Christ himself, teacher, shepherd and priest, and act as his representatives (*in eius persona*)" (LG 21 with n. 22, where the respective doctrine of the early Church is cited). Priests, as their helpers, also participate in their priestly office (LG 28; CD 28). They act *in persona Christi*. By means of the sacrament of orders and the character it imprints, they are configured to Christ and act in his name (PO 2, 6, 12; OT 8; SC 7).

After the Council, we find an increasing number of documents from the Roman curia which express the same fundamental ideas. The Congregation for Catholic Education, in its basic norms of 1970 for the formation of priests, explicitly underlined that, by means of sacred ordination, the priest becomes an "*alter Christus*".[3] The new Code of Canon Law of 1983 states in canon 1008: "By divine institution some among the Christian faithful are constituted sacred ministers through the sacrament of orders by means of the indelible character with which they are marked; accordingly they are consecrated and deputed to shepherd the people of God, each in accord with his own grade of orders, by fulfilling in the person of Christ [*in persona Christi*] the Head the functions of teaching, sanctifying and governing."

[3] AAS 62 (1970): no. 44.

John Paul II has from the outset of his pontificate occupied himself in a most forceful manner with the priesthood and the ministry of priests. Beginning in 1979, on Holy Thursday of every year he has addressed a message directly to priests. He repeatedly uses every opportunity—audiences, discourses and above all during the frequent priestly ordinations—to place the nature and essence of the priesthood in its correct theological and pastoral perspective. In this way the understanding of the priesthood is deepened.

The most important official act of this Pope on the priesthood was without doubt the convocation and realization of the Eighth Synod of Bishops, which had as its object the formation of priests. A central point of the discussions of the Synodal Fathers was without doubt the correct concept and genuine identity of the priest in the present world, especially in relation to the grave crisis in which the priest finds himself today. The culmination of this intensely studied question was the postsynodal apostolic exhortation, *Pastores dabo vobis*, which appeared on March 25, 1992, and dealt with the formation of priests in the context of their present situation.

In the second chapter of this apostolic exhortation, the Pope deals with "the nature and mission of the ministerial priesthood" and states expressly that the interventions of the Synodal Fathers "have shown an awareness of the specific ontological bond which unites the priesthood to Christ, the High Priest and Good

Shepherd" (11). The Pope concludes this exposition with a truly classic statement:

> The priest finds the full truth of his identity in being a derivation, a specific participation in and continuation of Christ himself, the one High Priest of the new and eternal Covenant. The priest is a living and transparent image of Christ the Priest. The priesthood of Christ, the expression of his absolute "newness" in salvation history, constitutes the one source and essential model of the priesthood shared by all Christians and the priest in particular. Reference to Christ is thus the absolutely necessary key for understanding the reality of priesthood (12, at end).

Based on this essential affinity between Christ and his priest, the theology of celibacy is not difficult to illustrate. John Paul II himself again gives us the key:

> It is especially important that the priest understand the theological motivation of the Church's law on celibacy. Inasmuch as it is a law, it expresses *the Church's will*, even before the will of the subject expressed by his readiness. But the will of the Church finds its ultimate motivation in the *link between celibacy and sacred Ordination*, which configures the priest to Jesus Christ the Head and Spouse of the Church. The Church, as the Spouse of Jesus Christ, wishes to be loved by the priest in the total and exclusive manner in which Jesus Christ her Head and Spouse loved her. Priestly celibacy, then, is the gift of self *in* and *with* Christ *to* his Church and

expresses the priest's service to the Church in and with the Lord (29).

An overview of the tradition of the Church can add to our understanding of the development of this theory. What will be said here concerning this has already been partly developed in our analysis of the evidence on clerical continence from the beginning of the Church. In presenting the evidence for the history of celibacy, reference to Sacred Scripture and its interpretation is of undoubted help to the theological arguments employed by the Synodal Fathers and the Holy Father. In the apostolic exhortation itself, we find many references to Sacred Scripture. The scriptural vision of celibacy has acquired even greater importance in light of recent studies.[4]

In the first written law known to us—canon 33 of the Council of Elvira—those bound by continence are clerics *positi in ministerio*, that is, those who serve at the altar. Further, the African canons continually speak of those who serve at the altar, handle the sacraments and administer them, those who, through their consecration, are obliged to chastity, which in turn ensures the efficacy of the prayers placed before God.

The first papal documents that deal with the obli-

---

[4] See in particular the historian B. Kötting, "Der Zölibat in der alten Kirche", in: *Schriften der Gesellschaft zur Förderung der westfälischen Wilhelmsuniversität zu Münster* 41 (Münster, 1970), and the theologian J. Galot, "Sacerdoce et célibat", in: *Gregorianum* 52 (1972): 731–57.

gation to celibacy are particularly important and in-
structive. We continually hear of two objections drawn
from Sacred Scripture which are refuted. The first is
the norm which Saint Paul gives to Timothy (1 Tim
3:2 and 3:12) and Titus (1:6): candidates, if married,
must be *unius uxoris viri*, or married only once (and
only to a virgin). Both Pope Siricius and Pope Innocent I repeatedly insist that this does not mean that
the candidate can live with the idea of begetting children. On the contrary, the regulation was established
because of the continence which had to be observed
in the future.

This official interpretation of a well-known passage
of Scripture, made by Popes and also adopted by councils, implies that those who feel the need to remarry
demonstrate by that fact that they are not able to live
the continence required for sacred ministers and therefore cannot be ordained. Thus, this passage from Scripture, far from being a support for marriage and its use
by clerics, is in fact a proof for continence, something
that was already demanded by the apostles. This interpretation remained valid during the following centuries. Thus the *Glossa Ordinaria* to the *Decretum* of
Gratian, that is, the commentary commonly accepted
for this text (beginning of Dist. 26), explains that there
are four reasons why a bigamist cannot be ordained.
Three reasons of a more spiritual nature are followed by
a fourth practical one, which states: because it would
be a sign of incontinence if one had passed from one

wife to another. Already in the thirteenth century, the great Decretalist Hostiensis (Henry of Susa) had explained in his commentary on the *Decretals* of Gregory IX (X, 1, 21, 3 ad v. alienum): the third reason of the four for this prohibition is "because one must fear incontinence".

That this interpretation of *unius uxoris vir* was also known and accepted in the East is clearly shown by the historian of the ancient Church Eusebius of Caesarea, who as has been pointed out was present at the Council of Nicaea and was sympathetic to the Arians. One would have thought that he would have leapt to the defense of the use of marriage by priests already married. But he expressly says that, in comparing the priest of the Old Testament with the priest of the New Testament, one compares corporal with spiritual generation and that the sense of the *unius uxoris vir* consists in this, that is, that those who have been consecrated and dedicated to the service of the divine cult must therefore properly abstain from sexual relations with their wives.[5]

This prohibition on the part of the Apostle Paul, that no bigamist can be admitted to sacred orders, has been strictly observed throughout the centuries and is still found among the irregularities for orders in the 1917 Code of Canon Law (can. 984, 4). In the classic period of canon law it was held that the dispensation

---

[5] *Demonstratio evangelica* 1:9: PG 22, 82.

of this prohibition was not possible, not even on the part of the Supreme Pontiff, because not even he could dispense *contra apostolum*, that is to say, against Sacred Scripture.[6]

It is also worth noting that the celibacy legislation of Trullo, canon 3, maintains this prohibition for priests, deacons and subdeacons, namely, that the candidates to these orders cannot have been married to a widow or with someone who had already been married once. On this point the Fathers of Trullo only wanted to mitigate the severity of the Church of Rome by conceding to those who had sinned against the prohibition of bigamy the possibility of conversion and of penitence. If within the time limit set by the Synod they had renounced this marriage, they could have remained in the ministry. The illogical nature of canon 3 in comparison with canon 13, which permits to priests and deacons the use of marriage contracted before ordination, is explained only by the fact that this apostolic prohibition was also profoundly anchored in the Eastern tradition, but without taking into account its true original meaning. We have here another tacit proof and guarantee for the authentic original meaning of complete continence after ordination as it remained alive in the Western Church and whose obser-

[6] Cf. the work of Stephan Kuttner, "Pope Lucius and the Bigamous Archbishop of Palermo", in: *Variorum Reprints*: Stephan Kuttner, *The History of Ideas and Doctrines of Canon Law in the Middle Ages* (London, 1980) 409–54.

vance was always faithfully accepted by the Church of Rome.

In this context it is worth mentioning two other texts from Scripture, which are not explicitly found in the early evidence. In fact the second of them is used today as an argument against the continence of the apostles themselves.

Among the qualities that Saint Paul demands in the minister of the Church, it is requested that he ought also to be ἐγκρατής, or continent. This term signifies sexual continence as is seen from the parallel text in which Saint Paul asks that for the sake of prayer spouses be continent.[7]

The second text of Sacred Scripture is found in 1 Corinthians 9:5 where Saint Paul affirms that he also would have had the right to have had a woman with himself as did the other apostles, the brothers of the Lord and Cephas. Many interpret this "woman" as a "wife" of the apostles, which indeed for Peter would have been true. But one needs to take into account that Paul does not speak simply of a γυναῖκα, who could well be a wife. Certainly not unintentionally Saint Paul adds the word ἀδελφήν, or "sister", in order to exclude any misunderstanding.

This fact has added weight if we consider that hence-

[7] Cf. Titus 1:8 and 1 Cor 7:9. According to the *Theol. Wörterbuch zum Neuen Testament*, ed. by Gerhard Kittel, 2 (Stuttgart, 1935): 338–40, this word is first used by Saint Paul and after him has the meaning of continence in an ethical sense and as a concept of virtue.

forth all the most important evidence touching on the continence of sacred ministers continually points out that, when one speaks of the wife of such ministers in the context of consequent sexual continence, the word *soror*, sister, is always used. The relationship between the spouses after the ordination of the husband is seen as that of brother and sister. Saint Gregory the Great remarks: "The priest from the moment of his ordination will love his priestess (that is, his wife) as a sister."[8] The Council of Gerona (517) decided that "if those who were previously married have been ordained, they must not live together as if they were spouses, for she who was a spouse has become a sister."[9] And the Second Council of Auvergne (535) establishes in its turn: "If a priest or a deacon has received the order of divine service, the husband immediately becomes a brother to his former wife".[10] This particular use of the words is found in many patristic and conciliar texts.

It is important that we now consider another point that is often invoked as an argument against the continence of ministers in the first centuries. An appeal is made to the Old Testament, in which it was licit, in fact a duty, to exercise the full use of marriage dur-

---

[8] *Dialoghi*, bk. 4, c. 11; PL 77, 336.

[9] Can. 6: Hermann Theodor Bruns, *Canones Apostolorum et Conciliorum sæc. IV–VII*, 2 (Berlin, 1839), 19.

[10] C. 13: *Corpus Christianorum*, Series Latina 148 A (Turnhout, 1974): 108.

ing the period in which the priests and Levites lived in their own house, free from service in the Temple. Normally we find a double response to this objection. In the first place, the priesthood of the Old Testament was entrusted to a tribe, which necessarily meant that the tribe had to continue thereby rendering marriage necessary. In addition, it is pointed out that the priesthood of the New Testament does not consist in familial descent.

There is a further, more important argument that is constantly repeated to underline the difference between the two priesthoods. The ministry of the priests of the Old Testament was limited to their time of service in the Temple, while the priests of the New Testament are involved in a continuous and uninterrupted ministry. This has therefore meant that the temporal obligation of celibacy and of purity of the Old Covenant has been extended to the unlimited and constant observance of the New. A further illustration is found in the passage of Saint Paul to the Corinthians (1 Cor 7:5), in which the apostle counsels spouses: "Do not refuse each other except by mutual consent, and then only for an agreed time, to leave yourselves free for prayer."

The priests of the New Covenant must instead pray continuously and dedicate themselves to their daily and constant ministry, in which, through their hands, the grace of baptism is given and the Body of Christ offered. Sacred Scripture teaches them to be completely pure in the exercise of this ministry, and the Fathers order them to preserve bodily continence.

The same documents, however, suggest yet another pastoral reason: How can a priest preach integrity and continence to a virgin or a widow if he himself gives greater importance to the begetting of children for the world rather than for God?

These considerations lead us to an understanding of the priesthood of the New Testament which is modeled on the will of Christ and substantially different from that of the Old Testament. The latter is understood in functional terms, limited in time and essentially external in nature. The priesthood of the New Testament, instead, involves the very nature of the person and therefore the whole man; as priest, the totality of his being is fundamentally involved in all his ministry. Christ wants the soul, heart and body of his priests; throughout his ministry, he wants that purity and continence that are a sign that he lives no longer according to the flesh but according to the spirit (Rom 8:8). The functional Levitical priesthood of the Old Testament can therefore never be a model of that priesthood of the New Testament, ontologically configured to Christ. There is a fundamental and essential difference between the two.

Thus, those men who have accepted the salvific message of Christ have from the very beginning understood that challenge of Christ to his apostles, that they must renounce even marriage for the sake of the kingdom of heaven (Mt 19:12) and that a disciple in the strict sense must also leave father, mother, wife, children, brother and sister (Lk 18:29; 14:26). It is in this context, especially in its significance for ecclesiastical celibacy, that one can readily understand the words of Saint Paul concerning the relationship to God of those who are unmarried, which is different from the relationship of those who are married (1 Cor 7:32–33).

It was to be the task of the scholars of the classical period of canon law, from the twelfth century on, to establish, explain and develop the reasons for the connection between continence and the priesthood of the New Testament. In the history of this scholarly development, already briefly described in the second part, we have pointed out how they found it difficult to establish and explain a satisfactory theory. While the Fathers had already understood that continence belonged to the essence of the priesthood—for example, when Epiphanius of Salamis stated that its charism consists in continence; or Saint Ambrose, that the obligation of continual prayer is the commandment of the New Covenant—the glossators were unable to create a theology of celibacy because they were not in fact theologians. In their works concerning the discipline of celibacy in the West, they were also very much conditioned by that of the East, the legitimacy of which they accepted as genuine, since they recognized both the legend of Paphnutius as well as the legislation of Trullo.

On the other hand, basing themselves on texts of the Western Catholic Church, they sought to create a theory which contained those essential elements necessary for a valid theology. Above all they understood that continence stands in a strict relationship with the *ordo sacer* and that this law had been established in the Church *propter ordinis reverentiam*, for the reverence which is due to orders; however they also understood continence as being connected to the order itself rather than to the man to be ordained.

From the synthesis developed by Saint Raymund of Peñafort, it is clear that the real motive for clerical continence was at that time, not the cultural purity of the minister of the altar, but rather the efficacy of mediatory prayer by the sacred minister. This was centered on a total dedication to God, on the real possibility of praying constantly as well as being completely free for pastoral ministry and for the service of the Church.

While it is true that the idea of the priesthood of the New Testament was not neglected in the theology of the succeeding centuries, it has only been the most recent crisis involving priests and vocations to the priesthood, especially in the second half of this century, that has urgently required a significant reappraisal of this argument.

The basis for this was established by the Second Vatican Council. In addition, from the very beginning of his pontificate, the Pope has continually made it the particular object of his doctrinal and pastoral program.

In this sense, it is significant that, even in his first message to priests on the occasion of Holy Thursday, he said, with respect to priestly celibacy, that the Western Church has always desired it and desires it also in the future inasmuch as "it is inspired by the example of our Lord Jesus Christ himself, the apostolic doctrine and all the tradition proper to it."[11] In the following years, he has continually returned to the theme of the priesthood and to celibacy. At the same time he has been determined to limit careless dispensations in this matter.

The high point of this pastoral concern and care was without doubt the convocation of the Eighth Synod of Bishops in October 1990, in which the question of priestly formation was dealt with in the context of its actual contemporary situation. This was done exhaustively through the contributions of representatives of the world episcopate and found its fullest expression in the apostolic exhortation *Pastores dabo vobis*. We can now rightly speak of a *Magna Charta* of the theology of the priesthood which will continue to be authoritative for the future of the Church.

It is not possible, nor indeed is it within the scope of this historical study, to offer a complete study of this apostolic text.[12] On the other hand, it does offer us the opportunity of presenting a final reflection on the

---

[11] AAS 71 (1979): 406.

[12] More recent reflections on the priesthood that preceded the apos-

theology of the celibate priesthood, which is intimately connected with the theology of the priesthood itself.

The final reason for the celibate priesthood is based on the will of the Church herself, which finds its motivation "in the link between celibacy and sacred ordination, which configures the priest to Jesus Christ, the head and spouse of the Church" (29). These words can be considered the central nucleus of the theology of celibacy which has been developed in the apostolic exhortation and which has been offered as the foundation for further development, study and consideration. At the very beginning of this study, we sought to indicate the elements of the theology of celibacy which were already apparent in the tradition but which had not been sufficiently developed. We are now in a position to assert that, in the presentation of the apostolic exhortation, we see that not only all these elements have been accepted and systematically developed but that other aspects which were not considered have also been utilized.

Above all we need to consider what was developed in chapter three, particularly numbers 22 and 23, on "Configuration to Christ, the Head and Shepherd, and

---

tolic exhortation are also useful especially given the theological competence of their authors. I refer here to the book by Cardinal Joseph Ratzinger, *Zur Gemeinschaft gerufen, die Kirche heute verstehen* (Freiburg, 1991), 98–123. In this chapter he deals with the question of the essence of the priesthood.

Pastoral Charity". Christ appears here in the sense of Ephesians 5:23–32, namely, as Spouse of the Church and the Church as the unique Bride of Christ. In connection with other scriptural passages, it presents a profound mystical theology of Christ and the Church in which the priest is immediately placed: "The priest is called to be the living image of Jesus Christ the Spouse of the Church. . . . In his spiritual life, therefore, he is called to live out Christ's spousal love towards the Church." The priest is therefore not without spousal love, he has as his Bride the Church.

> Therefore, the priest's life ought to radiate this spousal character which demands that he be a witness to Christ's spousal love, and thus be capable of loving people with a heart which is new, generous and pure, with genuine self-detachment, with full, constant and faithful dedication and at the same time with a kind of "divine jealousy" (cf. 2 Cor 11:2)—and even with a kind of maternal tenderness, capable of bearing "the pangs of birth" until "Christ be formed" in the faithful (cf. Gal 4:19).
>
> The internal principle, the force which animates and guides the spiritual life of the priest, inasmuch as he is configured to Christ the head and shepherd, is *pastoral charity*, as a participation in Jesus Christ's own pastoral charity.

The essential content of this "is *the gift of self*, the total gift of *self to the Church*, following the example of Christ. . . . With pastoral charity, which distinguishes the exercise of the priestly ministry as an *amoris offi-*

cium, 'the priest, who welcomes the call to ministry, is in a position to make this a loving choice, as a result of which the Church and souls become his first interest.' "

CONCLUSION

THE PRIESTHOOD OF THE CATHOLIC CHURCH is a mystery which is, in its turn, immersed in the mystery of the Church of Christ. Every problem concerning this priesthood—and especially the great and ever-present problem of celibacy—can and must not be resolved on the basis of considerations and reasons which are purely anthropological, psychological or sociological, or in terms which are in general profane and of this world. The problem of celibacy cannot be resolved within purely secular categories. Every aspect of the life and activity of the priest, his nature and his identity, is founded first of all on a theological justification. We have attempted to understand and develop the reality of clerical celibacy on the basis of its history as well as a developing theological reflection concerning it.

It follows in the very first place, at least under a formal aspect, that no satisfactory explanation for such a ministry is found in what we might term profane language. Rather it demands a language that corresponds to the mystery itself. In addition, if we take into account the actual nature of the Catholic priesthood, it is not enough simply to consider that which will render the Church herself more functionally effective: preserving or abandoning celibacy. The priesthood of the

New Testament is not a functional concept, as was that of the Old Testament, but is rather an ontological concept, and it is only on this basis that the proper means of acting can be derived, according to the axiom: *agere sequitur esse* (action follows being).

Given this theology of the New Testament priesthood, which has also been confirmed and deepened by the official Magisterium of the Church, we must ask ourselves if the basis of celibacy is to be actually found in its "suitability". Rather, is it not in fact really necessary and indispensable to the priesthood? Is there not a clear link between celibacy and priesthood? It is only by correctly responding to these questions that one can then consider whether the Church can decide one day to modify the obligation to celibacy or in fact to abolish it.[1]

We must nonetheless recognize that the Catholic priesthood, founded by Christ, is not based on the changing human circumstances but on the immutable mystery of the priest and the Church and of Christ himself.

[1] Cf. Winfried Leinweber, "Der Streit um den Zölibat im 19 Jahrhundert", as abstracted in *Klerikusblatt, Zeitschrift für Kleriker in Bayern und der Pfalz* 69 (1989): 254, or Josef Arquer, in: *Plädoyer für die Kirche* (Aachen: mm Verlag, 1991), 292.